PAINES PLOUGH

in association with **The Peter Wolff Theatre Trust** presents

SPLENDOUR

by **Abi Morgan**

Originally commissioned by Paines Plough
with Granada TV writers AWARD.
First performed at the Traverse Theatre 3 August 2000

SPLENDOUR

by **Abi Morgan**

Cast

Micheleine Mary Cunningham
Kathryn Faith Flint
Genevieve Myra McFadyen
Gilma Eileen Walsh

Director Vicky Featherstone
Designer Neil Warmington
Lighting Designer Nigel J Edwards
Original Music and Sound Nick Powell

Production Manager Alison Ritchie
Company Stage Manager (Edinburgh) Jessica Richards
Technical Stage Manager Pelham Warren
Props Buyer Keith Dunne

Publicity Photograph Rose Jones
Production Photography Manuel Harlan
Set Construction David & Sarah Holland
Press Representatives Cameron Duncan PR – 020 7636 3750
Leaflet/Poster & Cover Design Eureka! Design Consultants Ltd
Producer Hetty Shand

The performance lasts approximately one hour and twenty minutes
without an interval.

THE COMPANY

Abi Morgan – Writer

Abi has written for theatre, film, television and radio and currently has several projects in development. Her first two part original drama for TV, *My Fragile Heart* will be broadcast in Autumn 2000.

Her first play *Skinned* was performed by the Southampton Nuffield Theatre and Chelsea Centre in 1998 (shortlisted for the Allied Domecq new play award); *Sleeping Around*, a co-written play with Hilary Fannin, Stephen Greenhorn and Mark Ravenhill (Paines Plough); *Fast Food* (Royal Exchange Manchester, 1999) which was nominated for a best new play, Manchester Evening News Award; and *The Moment Is A Gift*, a collaboration with PRADA and Paines Plough in 1999. A similar collaboration, *Fortunes*, has just been performed in Milan.

She is currently under commission from The Royal Exchange, Canadian Stage, Birmingham Rep and will be working on a collaboration between Paines Plough and Frantic Assembly next year. *Splendour* was commissioned under Paines Plough/Granada Award Scheme.

Mary Cunningham – Micheleine

Theatre includes: *The White Devil*, *Man is Man* (Contact Theatre Manchester); *Juno And The Paycock* (Victoria Theatre, Stoke); *Breezeblock Park* (Liverpool Playhouse); *True West* (Crucible Theatre, Sheffield); *Cabaret*, *A Midsummer Night's Dream* (Everyman, Liverpool); a one woman play *Shouting At The Radio* at the Library Theatre, Manchester; *The Glass Menagerie*; *The Importance of Being Earnest*; *Talking Heads*; *Possession* (The Octagon, Bolton).

TV includes: *Coronation Street*; *Children's Ward*; *Sherlock Holmes* (Granada TV); *Scully*; *Brookside*; *And The Beat Goes On* (Channel 4); *Heartbeat*; *Where The Heart Is* (YTV); *Hercule Poirot* (LWT); *Hearts And Minds* (Witzend Productions); *Making Out* (BBC); *Touching Evil* (Meridian).

Nigel J Edwards – Lighting Designer

Recent work includes: *Riddance*, *The Cosmonaut's Last Message To The Woman He Once Loved In The Former Soviet Union*, *Crave*, *Sleeping Around* (Paines Plough); *Scar Stories*, *Disco Relax*, *Who Can Sing a Song To Unfrighten Me?*, *Dirty Work*, *Pleasure*, *Showtime*, *Speak Bitterness*, *Hidden J.*, *Club of no Regrets*, *Emmanuelle*, *Enchanted*, *Marina and Lee* (Forced Entertainment); *Victoria*, *Shadows*, *The Mysteries*, *Roberto Zucco* (RSC); *The Oresteia* (RNT); *Jenufa* (WNO); *The Maids* (ENO at the Lyric Theatre Hammersmith); *4:48 Psychosis* and *Cleansed* by Sarah Kane, *Bailengaire* (Royal Court); *The Maids* (Young Vic); *The Ballad of Yachiyo* (The Gate); *...love songs in a lonely desert full of crying men and howling women* (Anatomy).

Vicky Featherstone – Director

Vicky Featherstone is Artistic Director of Paines Plough. For Paines Plough: *Riddance* by Linda McLean (Fringe First & Herald Angel), *The Cosmonaut's Last Message To The Woman He Once Loved In The Former Soviet Union* by David Greig, *Crave* by Sarah Kane, *Sleeping Around* by Stephen Greenhorn, Hilary Fannin, Abi Morgan and Mark Ravenhill, and *Crazyhorse* by Parv Bancil.

She has directed *Outside Now* by David Greig, *The Moment Is A Gift That's Why It's Called The Present* by Abi Morgan, *Too Cold For Snow* by Michael Wynne, and most recently *Fortune* by Abi Morgan, David Greig, Michael Wynne & Danny Brown, for Prada as part of Milan Fashion Week.

She directed *Anna Weiss* for the Traverse Theatre(Fringe First and Scotland on Sunday's Critic's awards). Other work includes; script development for United Film and Television Productions where she created *Where The Heart Is* and developed *Touching Evil*. She is currently Script Development Executive for Granada Television Drama.

Faith Flint – Kathryn

Theatre includes: Award-winning *Handbag* by Mark Ravenhill, *The Belle Vue* (ATC); *Perfect Wedding*, *Volcano* (The Palace Theatre, Westcliffe); *Arabian Nights* (Magnificent Theatre Co.); *Beautiful Animals* (Mu-Lan Theatre Company); *Adam Bede* (Wolsey Theatre, Ipswich); *School For Wives* (national tour); *Essex Girls*, *Corner Boys* (both Royal Court Theatre Upstairs); *The Beaux Stratagem* (ETT, national tour); *Separate Tables* (national tour); *Toys For The Boys* (Yorkshire Theatre Co.); *Hang* (Royal National Studio); *Up And Under*, *The Changeling*, *Henceforward*, *My Children My Africa*, *She Stoops To Conquer* (all Harrogate Rep Company).

Faith's TV credits include: *Casualty*, *Navy In Action*, *Eastenders*, *The December Rose* (BBC); *Rides* (Warner Sisters/BBC); *Noah's Ark* (Whitehall Films) and *The Bill* (Thames TV). Films include: *Oktober* (Carnival Films); *Paddington Station* (Paddington Films) and *Shining Through* (20th Century Fox).

Myra McFadyen – Genevieve

Trained at RSAMD, Glasgow University and Ecole Jacques Lecoq. Theatre includes: *A Midsummer Night's Dream* (York Theatre Royal); *The Cone Gatherers*, *Antigone* and *Mary Queen of Scots Got Her Head Chopped Off* (Communicado Theatre Co & Donmar Warehouse); *The Guid Sisters* (Tron Theatre and Toronto Festival); *Bondagers*, *The Cow Jumped Over the Moon* and *Ines de Castro* (Traverse Theatre & Riverside, London); *A Winter's Tale* (Royal Exchange, Manchester); *As You Like It* (Royal Lyceum, Edinburgh); *The Rose Tattoo* (Theatr Clwyd) and numerous productions with Wildcat Stage Productions: *Talk of the Steamie*

(Greenwich); *Anything For A Quiet Life* (Almeida). For the Royal National Theatre: *Le Bourgeois Gentilhomme*, *Square Rounds*, *Macbeth*, *Bonjour la Bonjour* and *Out Of a House Walked a Man*; *Tartuffe* (Royal Exchange, Manchester); *Happy Days* (Tramway, Glasgow and Traverse Theatre); *Everyman*, *The Mysteries*, *The Winter's Tale* and *The Lion the Witch and the Wardrobe* (RSC).

TV includes: *Sweet Nothings*, *You've Never Slept in Mine*, *Laugh? I Nearly Paid My Licence Fee*, *The Killing Time* (BBC); *Blood Red Roses* (Freeway Films/Channel 4); *The Steamie* (STV); *Anything For A Quiet Life* (Holmes/Channel 4/Complicite); *Ines de Castro* (Nile Pictures/BBC) and *Put on By Cunning* (TVS). Film: *Rob Roy*. Myra has also directed: *Sacred Heart* (Communicado) and *On Yer Bike* (Citizens Theatre, Glasgow).

Nick Powell – Original Music & Sound

Nick has been working as a musician since 1990. He has toured and recorded with various bands including *Strangelove* (EMI Records), *Astrid* (Nude Records), *The Blue Aeroplanes* (Beggars Banquet) and *Witness* (Island Records). He has written music for TV, radio and short films for Channel Four, ITV, BBC World Service, Sky One and CBS in the US. As Musical Director of Suspect Culture – a theatre company formed in collaboration with Graham Eatough and David Greig – he has scored and been part of the development of eight shows including *Airport*, *Timeless*, *Mainstream* and this years tour of *Candide 2000*, as well as numerous workshops and performances in Britain and throughout Europe. Through the British Council, he has worked with Teatro De La Jacara in Madrid, Bouge-de-la and The Max Factory. He is one half of the duo OSKAR who have recently worked with Vicky Featherstone on three shows for PRADA in Milan, and have several CD releases in progress.

Jessica Richards – Company Stage Manager (Edinburgh)

Jess enjoyed six years as Company Stage Manager and occasionally performer with Communicado Theatre Company. Most recently she has worked with Quarantine on *Seesaw* at the Tramway and as a researcher and programme maker on *The F Word* (STV).

Eileen Walsh – Gilma

Eileen's theatre credits include: *Troilus and Cressida* (Oxford Stage Company); *Boomtown* (Rough Magic/Dublin Theatre Festival); *Disco Pigs*, for which she won the Edinburgh Fringe Festival Acting Excellence Award in 1997 (Bush Theatre/The Arts Theatre, London); *Phaedra's Love* (Corcadorca) and *Danti Dan* (Rough Magic/Hampstead Theatre).

Eileen's film credits include: *Miss Julie* (Mike Figgis); *Janice Beard 45wpm*, for which she was nominated as Best Newcomer by the British Independent Film Awards (Claire Kilner/Dakota Films) and *The Van* (Stephen Frears).

Neil Warmington – Designer

Recent work includes: *Crazyhorse*; *Riddance* (Paines Plough); *Marriage of Figaro* (Garsington Opera); *Full Moon for a Solemn Mass* (Traverse/Barbican Pit); *Desire Under the Elms*; *Jane Eyre* (Shared Experience); *Don Juan*; *Taming of the Shrew* (English Touring Theatre); *Family*; *Passing Places*; *King of the Fields* (Traverse Theatre); *Dissent*; *Angels in America* (7:84); *The Glass Menagerie*; *Comedians* (Royal Lyceum, Edinburgh); *Life is a Dream*; *Fiddler on the Roof* (West Yorkshire Playhouse); *The Duchess of Malfi* (Bath Theatre Royal); *Henry V* (Royal Shakespeare Company); *Much Ado About Nothing* (Queen's, London); *The Life of Stuff* (Donmar Warehouse); *Much Ado about Nothing*; *Waiting For Godot* (Liverpool Everyman); *The Tempest* (Contact, Manchester); *Women Laughing* (Watford); *Troilus & Cressida* (Opera North); *Oedipus Rex* (Connecticut State Opera). Neil recently designed Glasgow's 1999 Year of Architecture Launch and his awards include: 3 TMA Awards for best design (*Life is a Dream*; *Passing Places*; *Jane Eyre*); The Linbury Prize for Stage Design and The Sir Alfred Munnings Florence Prize for painting. Currently designing *Love's Labours Lost* (English Touring Theatre).

Pelham Warren – Technical Stage Manager

Trained at Bristol Old Vic Theatre School, Pelham has worked at the Theatre Royal Bath and Salisbury Playhouse. Most recently he worked with Sphinx Theatre Company and the Soul Train.

PAINES PLOUGH

'Paines Plough has discovered a rich seam of talent'

The Independent '99

Paines Plough has been discovering outstanding new voices in British Theatre for twenty-five years. Funded by the Arts Council of England, Paines Plough produces two new plays a year and tours them throughout the UK. Since the driving force behind the company has always been the vision of the playwright, we have created a programme of work to access, support and develop the most exciting voices nationally.

Since Vicky Featherstone's appointment as the fifth Artistic Director in 1997 we have produced *Riddance* by Linda McLean, which won a Fringe first and a Herald Angel award, *The Cosmonaut's Last Message to the Woman he Once Loved in the Former Soviet Union* by David Greig, *Crave* by Sarah Kane, *Sleeping Around* by Hilary Fannin, Stephen Greenhorn, Abi Morgan and Mark Ravenhill, *Crazyhorse* by Parv Bancil and *The Wolves* by Michael Punter.

> *'Over the last three years, the company has grown by over 100%... Featherstone has turned herself into a major force. The more successful she is, the better and more daring she has become as a director.'*

The Guardian '99

TICKET TO WRITE funded by the national lottery, is our nation-wide playwriting programme. A partnership between Paines Plough and four major regional theatres; it finds, commissions and produces the best new writing talent in those regions. Through this programme Paines Plough have discovered, commissioned and developed 40 new writers and so far produced and toured 30 short plays. TICKET TO WRITE is now its final phase with the West Yorkshire Playhouse and we will produce ten short plays by black and Asian writers from Yorkshire this Autumn.

WILD LUNCH is a festival of script-in-hand performances. Born out of a selected writers group, the latest festival Jubilee – Plays from Underground, was presented in collaboration with the BBC New Writing Initiative. One of these plays *Stratford* by Debbie Green is being produced by Paines Plough and presented at the Soho Theatre in October 2000 as part of their Autumn lunchtime season.

Coming Soon

In Spring 2001 the company will present Gary Owen's first play *Crazy Gary's Mobile Disco* in conjunction with the Welsh new writing company Sgript Cymru. Later in the year Paines Plough will collaborate with the much acclaimed Frantic Assembly on a new play by Abi Morgan.

THE PETER WOLFF THEATRE TRUST

The Peter Wolff Theatre Trust is delighted to be supporting *Splendour* by Abi Morgan.

The trust was founded by Peter Wolff, a textile entrepreneur, who has had a great love of the British theatre all his life. In January 1998 he created the non-profit-making Trust to encourage the work of emerging British playwrights and to bring these plays to a wider audience.

This year the Trust is also delighted to support:

Be My Baby by Amanda Whittington at The Soho Theatre

The Good Samaritan by David Haig at Hampstead Theatre

To The Green Fields Beyond by Nick Whitby at The Donmar Warehouse

The Trust welcomes submissions for original projects seeking support. The Director of the Trust is Neal Foster and individual playwrights and theatre companies should contact Neal Foster at The Peter Wolff Theatre Trust, Suite 612, 162 Regent Street, London W1R 5TB. Telephone: 020 7494 4662.

PAINES PLOUGH

Vicky Featherstone
Artistic Director

Hetty Shand
Acting Administrative Director

Belinda Hamilton
Administrative Director

Caroline Newall
Administrator

Jessica Dromgoole
Literary Manager

Lucy Morrison
Special Projects

PAINES PLOUGH
4th Floor
43 Aldwych
London WC2B 4DN

Tel: +44 (0) 20 7240 4533
Fax: +44 (0) 20 7240 4534

Email: office@painesplough.com

Funded by THE ARTS COUNCIL OF ENGLAND

SPLENDOUR

TOUR DATES

3 – 26 August
Traverse Theatre
Edinburgh Fringe Festival 2000

12 – 16 September
The Drum
Plymouth Theatre Royal

18 – 19 September
Exeter Phoenix

21 – 23 September
Liverpool Everyman

26 September
Darlington Arts Centre

27 – 28 September
Live Theatre Newcastle

30 September
Windsor Arts Centre

3 – 4 October
Leicester Haymarket Studio

5 – 7 October
Salberg Studio
Salisbury Playhouse

10 – 11 October
The Bull, Barnet

13 – 14 October
Stephen Joseph Theatre,
Scarborough

18 – 19 October
Komedia, Brighton

20 – 21 October
Bolton Octagon Theatre

24 –25 October
Old Town Hall Hemel Hempstead

26 October
Arena Theatre, Wolverhampton

27 – 28 October
Cambridge Drama Centre

31 October – 1 November
Warwick Arts Centre

2 – 4 November
Ustinov Studio
Bath Theatre Royal

First published in 2000 by Oberon Books Ltd.
(incorporating Absolute Classics)
521 Caledonian Road, London N7 9RH
Tel: 020 7607 3637 / Fax: 020 7607 3629
e-mail: oberon.books@btinternet.com

A catalogue record for this book is available from the British
Library.

ISBN: 1 84002 189 6

Cover photograph: Rose Jones

Cover design: Eureka! Design Consultants Ltd

Printed in Great Britain by Antony Rowe Ltd, Reading.

Characters

MICHELEINE
the wife, female, late 40s

GILMA
the interpreter, female, early/mid 20s

KATHRYN
the photographer, female, mid/late 30s

GENEVIEVE
the informer, female, early/mid 40s

Setting: The play is set in a house, in an affluent neighbourhood on the edge of a large city.

The sound of fireworks/shelling should be abstract.

A woman. MICHELEINE. Late 40s. Sassy. Elegant. A drink somewhere. Always near. GILMA. Mid 20s. Less well dressed. Stooped on the floor sweeping up something with a pan and brush. KATHRYN. Mid/late 30s. More robust. Absorbed in looking at a painting. GENEVIEVE. Early/mid 40s. Dressed as if in a rush. Hair wet, bag in hand, flushed from the outside. Pulling off a scarf as if she has just come from outside.

MICHELEINE: Genevieve, your hair it's –

GENEVIEVE: Snow.

KATHRYN: …dripping on her green dress.

GENEVIEVE: I'm fine. The roads are terrible.

>   *GILMA sweeps up on the floor.*

MICHELEINE: It's nothing, just a bit of glass. (*Introducing.*) Gilma.

GENEVIEVE: Gilma.

GILMA: Don't look me up and down like that.

GENEVIEVE: I had to take the back route. Is there anything to drink?

MICHELEINE: Yes. We're onto our third.

>   *GENEVIEVE walks across the room and pours herself a glass of vodka.*

>   I am sitting in a garden a few hours before this moment. My husband is to my left –

GENEVIEVE: Jesus –

MICHELEINE: …we are having lunch with friends.

GENEVIEVE: (*i.e. drink.*) …Micha, where did you get this?

MICHELEINE: Lunch with Isabella.

KATHRYN: We are drinking chilli vodka.

13

GENEVIEVE: You saw her?

MICHELEINE: A few hours ago.

KATHRYN: It is blindingly hot.

MICHELEINE: To my right is a pudgy man I always seem to get stuck with. He laughs too much at a joke my husband makes –

GILMA hands MICHELEINE back the dustpan and brush.

GILMA: (*To MICHELEINE.*) I'm sorry.

MICHELEINE: Of course, it's a very funny joke…

GENEVIEVE: I thought Oolio would be –

MICHELEINE: Coming. You know the office. You're dripping on the carp –

GENEVIEVE: (*To MICHELEINE.*) Micha, there are bells ringing all along the Southside.

A beat. GENEVIEVE clocks KATHRYN looking at the painting.

MICHELEINE: A nun is walking through a park when a giant gorilla attacks her. He ravishes her in the bushes and then quickly bounds away. Clearly distressed and returning to her convent her Mother Superior with some concern takes the young nun aside. 'My dear I can't help but notice, you seem very upset of late.'

GENEVIEVE: The painting –

GENEVIEVE comes up to look at the painting with KATHRYN.

I see you've noticed the painting.

KATHRYN: Sorry?

GENEVIEVE: The painting? You like it?

MICHELEINE: We commissioned it. It's not one of his best.

KATHRYN: I'm sorry… (*To GILMA.*) Gilma?
   (*To GENEVIEVE.*) I'm sorry. I don't understand.

MICHELEINE: (*Introducing.*) Kathryn.

KATHRYN: (*To GENEVIEVE.*) Kathryn.

MICHELEINE: (*To GENEVIEVE.*) She's a very important
   journalist.

KATHRYN: I've come to take a photograph.

MICHELEINE: This is my best friend, Genevieve. Our
   husbands have been, were friends for twenty –

GENEVIEVE: …five –

MICHELEINE: …years.

   GENEVIEVE and KATHRYN shake hands.

KATHRYN: Gilma?

GILMA: The painting. Her husband –

KATHRYN: …painted it? We're discussing fucking painting.

MICHELEINE: (*To KATHRYN.*) Won't you have a little nut?

Moved by the Mother Superior's vigilante concern, the
young nun confesses to the recent contretemps with the
gorilla in the park. The Mother Superior bestows
sympathy but as the weeks pass, a vow of silence is
shrouded over the terrible event. But one day the Mother
Superior, unable to contain herself, betrays a certain
curiosity, a certain girlish interest… 'My dear, don't
think me indiscreet, but may I ask did it hurt?' 'Of
course it hurt Mother Superior, I mean imagine this big
gorilla, he never rings, he never writes, there's not a –

Midway through the punch line, the pudgy man, who is
already laughing, suddenly shoots up and says… 'Ssh,
did you hear that?'

GILMA: (*To GENEVIEVE.*) The bells on the Southside.
I heard them, this afternoon.

MICHELEINE: 'Faint, on a cold breeze.' (*Beat.*) I heard
nothing at all.

GILMA: There were people, they were dancing –

MICHELEINE: No.

GILMA: (*To MICHELEINE.*) And soldiers being paraded.

GENEVIEVE: Micheleine –

GILMA: That is impossible. You must have been –

MICHELEINE: I must have been –

GILMA: …very far away.

KATHRYN: What did she say?

GILMA shakes her head.

MICHELEINE: I sat next to that pudgy man –

GENEVIEVE: Who laughs at almost anything?

MICHELEINE: Oolio did his usual –

GENEVIEVE: Not?

MICHELEINE: The gorilla and the nun.

MICHELEINE and GENEVIEVE laugh.

'Of course it hurt Mother Superior, I mean imagine this
big gorilla, he never rings, he never writes, there's not a
bunch of flowers in sight…'

And we're laughing but the truth is –

KATHRYN: Why the hell are they laughing?

MICHELEINE: …I want to but today –

GILMA: (*Touching GENEVIEVE.*) Fuck, you're freezing.

MICHELEINE: …I don't get the joke at all.

KATHRYN: I am standing in the foyer of a large hotel a few hours before this moment. In a city that is familiar, a city I have been to several times before. This job that I have come for, this job is particular. I have been travelling since five a.m. Greenwich Meantime. I am tired. At the airport there is no one to meet me. It's the usual. I pick up a taxi. The taxi is expensive, too expensive, I argue. I win my case.

MICHELEINE: This portrait of my husband?

GILMA: This portrait that you plan to take? You must be patient with him. He rarely courts press.

KATHRYN: It was agreed through your office.

GILMA: A request from his advisors. It was a personal invitation.

MICHELEINE: We're delighted you could come.

GILMA: (*To GENEVIEVE.*) It's snowing.

GENEVIEVE: Only a little now.

GILMA: …You drove along the…

GENEVIEVE: Past the Gymnasium…

GILMA: …I use to swim there as a child…

GENEVIEVE: Since they bombed the bridge last August it's the only route to take.

KATHRYN: I arrive at my hotel. There are large lions and a plastic flamingo arrangement in the foyer. The man in the lobby reassures me that they are not real. Reclaimed since the Zoo was bombed. There is frost on the lion's mane.

The phone rings.

MICHELEINE: Genie, your hair. I'll get you a towel.

MICHELEINE eats. The phone stops ringing.

KATHRYN: I ask if there have been any messages for me and a girl standing in the lobby, a girl wearing a coat that is clearly not hers, a girl wearing a coat that is weighed down with shoulder pads, a girl –

GILMA: (*To KATHRYN.*) From newspaper? Excuse me? You've come to take the photograph?

KATHRYN: …with an accent I can barely understand –

GILMA: I'm interpreter. The car's… You come? This way.

KATHRYN: (*To GILMA.*) My office?

GILMA: Yes. They contact me.

KATHRYN: They arranged for you to take me?

GILMA: (*To KATHRYN.*) Gilma.

KATHRYN: (*Nodding.*) Gilma. (*Beat.*) She barely understands me. In my mind I am sticking pins in the office PA.

MICHELEINE comes in, dropping a towel in GENEVIEVE's lap.

GENEVIEVE: Micha –

MICHELEINE: Genie, what are we to do with you?

GENEVIEVE: Was that Oolio on the telephone?

MICHELEINE: Yes, he's on his way. Gilma? A Northern name.

GILMA: Not always.

MICHELEINE: How's Darius?

GENEVIEVE: He called last week. I think there's a new girlfriend –

MICHELEINE: A girlfriend at last. We had money on it he was –

GENEVIEVE: And Marcus wrote. He's going to bring Gina and the children to stay.

MICHELEINE: (*Eyeing KATHRYN.*) She's watching me. (*Beat.*) That's good. That's lovely, Genie –

GILMA: Stockings –

MICHELEINE: Italian.

GILMA: With underwear I bet to match.

MICHELEINE: Gilma… I wonder I didn't clock that right away.

GILMA: (*To MICHELEINE.*) Nice glasses.

MICHELEINE: Siberian. (*Beat.*) Thank you.

GILMA: You're welcome.

MICHELEINE: That sounds very American.

GILMA: Sorry?

MICHELEINE: 'You're welcome'? (*Beat.*) That's very American.

GILMA: The University of California. I studied abroad.

KATHRYN holds up her bag to MICHELEINE.

KATHRYN: Is it okay, if I…? Gilma?

GILMA: Is it okay? To unpack her things?

MICHELEINE: Please tell her, of course –

GILMA: (*To KATHRYN.*) It's fine.

MICHELEINE: (*Calling out.*) Marianna… Will she need some help?

KATHRYN shakes her head.

GENEVIEVE: The painting is of the city. That is the river and that is the persons... I speak a little of your language...

KATHRYN: Someone should tell her very badly. (*Beat.*) The persons?

GENEVIEVE: Yes. The persons of the town.

KATHRYN: And which bit are the people?

GENEVIEVE: There are the persons.

KATHRYN: Right.

GENEVIEVE: You see their faces?

KATHRYN: I see. Yes. I see. Right. Is that a cow?

The phone rings. And rings.

MICHELEINE: (*Calling out.*) Marianna, Marianna, will you please get the telephone?

The phone stops ringing.

No matter. (*Calling out.*) Marianna. (*To herself.*) We need more ice.

MICHELEINE goes out.

GENEVIEVE: How did you get here?

GILMA/KATHRYN: Taxi.

GILMA: The office said you'd pay it.

KATHRYN: I know this is a lie. A blatant, shameless lie. The office have included it, she has already been paid once today.

GILMA: If there's going to be a problem –

KATHRYN: I reassure her there's not a problem, but I know the tricks they all readily have –

GILMA: It takes on average –

GENEVIEVE: Twenty minutes, fifteen if you're lucky.

GILMA: It's a forty-minute ride. It's better if we pay him. He won't drive us anywhere until he sees there's cash.

KATHRYN: He takes us on the scenic route. The view is one I'm used to, one we've all come to expect. (*Beat.*) She'll ask for forty and I'll know it will only cost twenty. She splits the extra and the driver gets the ride. (*Beat.*) And he will come back for us? For sure before midnight? The office are waiting?

> She nods. (*Beat.*) I don't trust her.

GILMA: (*Nodding.*) She's mean with her money.

KATHRYN: Her shoulder pads crunch as she climbs in the car.

GILMA: The driver is a friend, a friend of my brother's. He's a gambler and a user. I hold back ten. That way he'll come back. That way she won't criticise. Please do not worry. The door?

KATHRYN: Huh?

GILMA: Not closed.

KATHRYN: (*Beat.*) She leans across me and there is a faint smell of BO.

> *MICHELEINE comes through, a bucket of ice in her hand.*

MICHELEINE: Do you know I went out and found the front door wide open? We now have ice both inside and out. (*Holding up ice.*) Genevieve, you said the traffic –

GENEVIEVE: A log-jam all along the North route.

MICHELEINE: (*Beat.*) No one likes the cold nights. If I didn't know better, I'd say this snow's in to stay. Have you seen it outside?

KATHRYN: She lives…?

GENEVIEVE: Only five minutes away –

MICHELEINE: Her husband was –

GILMA: …The nuts are finished.

MICHELEINE: …a marvellous man.

GENEVIEVE: He died…

GILMA: Four years ago…

MICHELEINE: He painted the picture as a memory for us all.

GILMA: Under-wired, most definitely. With stockings and suspenders.

MICHELEINE: La Perla have the ones I normally prefer.

GENEVIEVE: (*To MICHELEINE.*) Have you called Angelica? (*Beat.*) Micheleine? She's at home with the baby boy?

MICHELEINE: Your accent it's…?

GILMA: Californian.

GENEVIEVE: California?

GILMA: Hollywood.

KATHRYN: Hollywood, my arse.

GILMA: It's beautiful.

KATHRYN: She's making chitchat.

GILMA: You've worked in America?

KATHRYN: Elections, a race riot, some bomber in Idaho, some coverage in South America. The Idaho bomber a few years ago.

GILMA: Idaho?

KATHRYN: In America.

GILMA: Yes, Hollywood.

KATHRYN: A1 wonderful. An interpreter who doesn't actually know how to interp. (*Beat.*) She's not even listening.

GILMA: (*Beat.*) I hear every word.

GILMA knocks her drink back too hard, coughs.

MICHELEINE: Careful –

GILMA: It just catches you –

MICHELEINE: …when you're least expecting –

Chilli, chilli vodka.

GILMA: Right at the back of/

MICHELEINE: …the back of the throat.

MICHELEINE hands her a glass of water.

(*Beat.*) Alright now?

GILMA: Thank you.

MICHELEINE: You're welcome.

GILMA: That's quite alright.

GENEVIEVE: (*i.e. drink.*) …Micha, where did you get this?

MICHELEINE: (*Beat.*) Lunch with Isabella. (*Beat.*) She insisted. She insisted I bring a bottle home.

'For the pain. The chilli? To enjoy the pain as you drink it.'

I knock back the last mouthful quickly, gently scalding my tongue. We won't forget this moment. We want you to know this. There's a sincerity that embarrasses me. Embarrasses my husband.

I pray he does not intervene with another joke.

Help me out, sweetheart. We have a little signal –

'Darling, your ulcer? We must get that ulcer home.'

My husband informs us, our car is surely waiting. It is as
we leave I notice –

❖

*GILMA is standing admiring a beautiful Venetian vase, red
and lilac catching in the light, roughly wrapped in newspaper
and rolling on its side.*

GILMA: It's beautiful.

MICHELEINE nods.

MICHELEINE: Venetian.

GILMA: The vase?

MICHELEINE: In Isabella's hallway, resting on a bookshelf.
A wedding present we gave them some years ago.

KATHRYN: She nods so lightly –

GILMA: So carelessly forgotten.

MICHELEINE: Isabella is a woman who guards possessions
carefully.

KATHRYN: …roughly wrapped in newspaper and rolling
on its side.

MICHELEINE: I am therefore surprised when she takes it
down from the shelf and offers it to me.

GILMA: A vase which I can see is worth half of what
I earned last month. A vase which at this moment,
I would dearly like to own. Red. Venetian. She's clearly
distracted… I wonder if she'd notice –

MICHELEINE: (*To GILMA.*) A gift.

*GILMA leans forward to touch the vase, turns, aware of
MICHELEINE watching her, withdraws her hand.*

MICHELEINE: 'Take it – we'd like you to have it.' Is it
my imagination or does our hostess shake as she holds it
out in her arms?

GILMA: …It would fit in my coat.

MICHELEINE: My smile is a graceful smile but as we stand
in her hallway I see there is pity in her husband's eyes.

The phone starts ringing.

Marianna, our –

GILMA: (*To KATHRYN.*) …housekeeper –

MICHELEINE: Don't worry, she normally answers it.

The phone stops ringing.

KATHRYN: That noise? What is it?

MICHELEINE: There's no breeze. The silence carries
everything.

GENEVIEVE: The door was wide open, I didn't think of
closing it, I thought she must be outside –

MICHELEINE: I forgot. (*Beat.*) It's her half – day.

He squeezes my hand and leans back to kiss me. Tells
me that there are papers at the office that he really must
sign. I am to go on alone, he'll be back quite shortly. I
clutch the half bottle of vodka and the vase from these
strangers. People we have known and loved for years.

Something about his manner. Something about his
manner… We pull through the gates and…

KATHRYN: We are here when she arrives.

MICHELEINE stands, a drink somewhere near. GILMA is once more on the floor sweeping up some glass with a dustpan and brush. KATHRYN is standing looking at the painting. GENEVIEVE now has her coat on, her hair still wet, pulling off her scarf. The repeat is as before only slightly faster.

MICHELEINE: Genevieve. (*Touching hair.*) Your hair, it's –

KATHRYN: …dripping on her green dress.

GENEVIEVE: I'm fine. The roads are terrible.

MICHELEINE: It's nothing, just a bit of glass. (*Introducing.*) Gilma –

GENEVIEVE: Gilma.

GILMA: Don't look me up and down like that.

GENEVIEVE: I had to take the back route. Is there anything to drink?

MICHELEINE: Yes, we're onto our third…

MICHELEINE offers KATHRYN a cigarette.

Do you mind?

KATHRYN shakes her head.

I'm giving up.

GENEVIEVE: Jesus, where did you get this?

MICHELEINE: Isabella.

GILMA: Marlboro. A brand new pack.

MICHELEINE: Genie, what are we to do with you? I'll get you a towel.

❖

KATHRYN: She is shorter than I expected and not as beautiful, certainly not as her photos have shown. Her behind is large and there is a thin line of hair bleached on her top lip. Her clothes are too tight and the handbag that she is carrying –

MICHELEINE: Prada. Last season's and shoes to match.

GILMA: Pink with tiny stripy edging. The soles look barely dirty. I pray. Yes indeedy they are my size. (*To MICHELEINE.*) Your shoes, they're very hairy.

KATHRYN: Animal not mineral. Possibly Zebra.

GILMA: She says she thinks you're wearing –

MICHELEINE: (*To GILMA.*) I really don't think so.

KATHRYN: If there's a seam, tell her, it's normally where the anus once was.

GILMA: (*To MICHELEINE.*) She likes them.

MICHELEINE: Please tell her thank you, I have many more.

KATHRYN: Amidst such devastation how do you…

GILMA: Devastation… To cause great destruction…

KATHRYN: (*Beat.*) I barely embarrass her.

GILMA: They're delivered by road.

KATHRYN: How many handbags –

MICHELEINE: …do I actually own? (*Beat.*) A number is not important.

GILMA: I'm glad I've worn my big coat, with very, very deep pockets.

MICHELEINE: A figure is just a crude way to define us all. I find it rather tasteless… This fascination with quantity.

GILMA: Twelve in each side and one larger pocket just under my arse.

MICHELEINE: Two maybe three…hundred. (*Beat.*) She asks too many questions.

I grace them by –

KATHRYN: …showing us the room where they are stored.

MICHELEINE: How can you quantify something that means nothing to one person and everything to another? A number is redundant.

MICHELEINE: (*To GENEVIEVE.*) I've been showing them my handbags.

KATHRYN's gaze falls to the painting beyond.

KATHRYN: On the wall is a painting. An obscene and gross painting. It is modern. In oils. Smeared like shit.

GENEVIEVE: (*Beat.*) I see you've noticed the painting, the painting on the wall?

KATHRYN: Gilma, can you tell her, the light, it's fading.

MICHELEINE: (*Beat.*) My husband… Will you explain to her…

GILMA: At the office…

KATHRYN: Yeah. I got that.

MICHELEINE: He's had to –

KATHRYN: …sign papers. Yeah. She said that before. (*Watching MICHELEINE.*) Her nails are aubergine, the colour of aubergine, and clasped around her bag even in her house. As if she is under threat, as if she is under threat or about to go somewhere.

GILMA: (*To GENEVIEVE.*) Fuck, you're freezing?

GENEVIEVE: My heating's jammed –

MICHELEINE: That car –

GENEVIEVE: It's a bit temperamental.

MICHELEINE: Genie, it's time to get rid of that car.

GILMA: …You drove along the…

GENEVIEVE: Past the Gymnasium…

MICHELEINE: The changing rooms are now offices and the athletic pitch barracks…

GENEVIEVE: Since they bombed the bridge last August –

GILMA: …It's the only route to take.

GENEVIEVE: (*To KATHRYN.*) Your first time here? Over here?

MICHELEINE: You must visit our coastal towns.

KATHRYN: (*To GILMA.*) I've been mainly…mainly in the Northern states.

MICHELEINE: (*To GENEVIEVE.*) Gilma's the interpreter, if you want to talk to –

KATHRYN: (*As if introducing herself.*) Kathryn.

MICHELEINE: …Kathryn, Genie, it's best if we all go through her.

KATHRYN: The piano?

MICHELEINE: My grandson –

GILMA: (*To KATHRYN.*) …has lessons here.

MICHELEINE: Tuesdays and Thursdays.

What am I doing? Shut up. Stop talking so much.

KATHRYN: I'll have to move it. The piano. Gilma?

MICHELEINE: (*To GILMA.*) Ask her, will you ask her…will I see the pictures first?

GILMA: The pictures, you'll send copies?

KATHRYN: The film will go on the first flight. I don't get to see –

MICHELEINE: He has a little disfigurement to the left of his face –

KATHRYN: The film goes ahead of me.

MICHELEINE: …he's naturally self-conscious. The removal of a mole.

GILMA: Shoot him from the left.

KATHRYN: It will depend on the light.

MICHELEINE: He's a man you admire?

KATHRYN: More fascinated.

GILMA: More fascinated.

MICHELEINE: (*Beat.*) To me he's my husband. The piano… Be careful. It is a Steinway.

A sound. Faint. Just audible. In the distance. Bells/shelling/ the rumble of guns.

He squeezes my hand and leans back to kiss me. A small patch of stubble… Back in one hour. Just give them a drink – Oolio… Oolio… He's already gone.

(*To GILMA.*) Your English. You learnt?

GILMA: In the university of California.

GENEVIEVE: California?

MICHELEINE: (*To GILMA.*) You're very lucky…

KATHRYN: California my arse. (*Watching MICHELEINE.*) She's nervous.

MICHELEINE: I'm shaking. The hostess' disease. The young girl is sly, her coat is quite terrible –

The older. Tougher. No ring. No man.

Kathryn, it is Kathryn who clocks my hands. God I need a drink.

KATHRYN: We move the piano.

MICHELEINE: Careful –

GILMA: We make a big great scratch as we drag it across the floor. If we're moving pianos I'm asking for more.

KATHRYN: On the stool is an imprint, a perfect crease, a perfect crease of a very tiny child's behind.

GILMA: Her grandson's.

MICHELEINE: He's this tall. A sweetheart. A tiny little sweetheart.

The ring of a phone. For a long time until –

Excuse me, a moment –

KATHRYN: She answers the telephone.

MICHELEINE: (*As if on the phone.*) Darling…

GENEVIEVE: She's talking to Oolio.

MICHELEINE: And ruining my floor. (*As if on the phone.*) She seems very nice. She's brought a lot of equipment. (*She laughs.*) I'll tell her… I'll tell her… (*To KATHRYN.*) He's making a joke.

GENEVIEVE: She laughs too much.

MICHELEINE: I laugh too much.

GILMA: Something funny at his office.

MICHELEINE: He says would you mind…

GILMA: Would we mind holding on?

❖

MICHELEINE pours three shots for them. They all chink glasses and knock back in one shot.

KATHRYN: Wow.

GILMA: Jesu –

MICHELEINE: I'm sorry I should have warned you.

KATHRYN: I like it.

GILMA: (*Coughing.*) Jesu –

KATHRYN: (*To GILMA.*) Are you okay?

MICHELINE: The first time I tried it, my husband had to slap me, hard.

MICHELINE hits GILMA between the shoulder blades.

I'll get you some water.

GILMA: It catches you –

MICHELEINE: Right at the back of –

GILMA: …the throat.

MICHELEINE hands her a glass of water.

MICHELEINE: (*Beat.*) Alright now?

GILMA: Thank you.

MICHELEINE: You're welcome.

GILMA: (*Beat.*) Nice glasses.

MICHELEINE: Siberian.

KATHRYN: (*Eyeing GILMA.*) I know what you're doing.

GILMA: (*Holding up glass.*) M for Micheleine.

MICHELEINE: A whim of my husbands. M on all the silverware.

GILMA: (*Admiring the glass.*) M that's very nice. If I could just get a set.

KATHRYN: Put it back, put it back, put it back –

❖

KATHRYN: Her children?

GILMA: They live near.

KATHRYN: The grandson with –

MICHELEINE: My daughter, Angelica.

GENEVIEVE: The girl translates.

MICHELINE: …touches everything.

GILMA: (*Beat.*) She's married to an obstetrician.

MICHELEINE: My son is studying –

GILMA: …at agricultural college –

MICHELEINE: …in the North. My daughter, Angelica, she lives on the Southside. How's Darius?

GENEVIEVE: Skiing. He's skiing with a new girlfriend.

MICHELEINE: (*Beat.*) A girlfriend. At last. We had money on it he was…

KATHRYN: The woman flinches.

GILMA: (*To KATHRYN.*) A daughter, a son, one grandson and the woman in the green dress –

GENEVIEVE: Two boys. They're all grown up –

GILMA: They don't live at home.

GENEVIEVE: Have you called Angelica? Micheleine?
Is she at home with the boy today?

GILMA: Two glasses. A lighter. Nail varnish and a light thing.

MICHELEINE: Don't worry so. Don't worry so.

GILMA: (*To GENEVIEVE.*) The bells on the Southside.
I heard them. This afternoon.

MICHELEINE: Where are you?

You worry too much.

GENEVIEVE: (*To MICHELEINE.*) There were people, they
were dancing and soldiers being paraded. If Angelica –

MICHELEINE: There is mud on my carpet.

GILMA: (*Picking up soles of feet.*) Fuck… You can't have not
heard it.

KATHRYN: …Gilma, your shoes…

MICHELEINE: Outside…outside…

KATHRYN: Gilma –

GILMA exits as if going outside.

GENEVIEVE: There have been bells ringing all day on the
Southside.

KATHRYN: Excuse me…do you mind?

KATHRYN holds up her mobile, as if about to make a call.

MICHELEINE: Genie, you exaggerate.

GENEVIEVE: The roads… There's a log-jam.

MICHELEINE: You're always prone to exaggerate.

GENEVIEVE: If Angelica's on the Southside…

KATHRYN on mobile.

GILMA: Inside, I can hear them talking, she is on the telephone... Screeching down the telephone. That woman, that woman has a pickle up her arse.

KATHRYN: Nick, it's Kathryn... Nick...can you hear me?

GILMA: In the taxi, on the way here I take her the long way.

KATHRYN: (*As if on the phone.*) It's the signal... Fuck it... I'm here... We've arrived... We're waiting for him... Apparently he's on his way... Nick... There's a lot of noise coming from the Southside.

GILMA: Down the main street there are fronts of houses, with no rooms only doorways. A boy, too big, too old sleeps in a pram in a hotel front door.

MICHELEINE: I am nervous. I talk.

GENEVIEVE: Too much.

KATHRYN: (*As if on phone.*) Nick... I can't hear you... Nick... Nick... No, he hasn't arrived yet...

GILMA: At a time like this I think of just leaving them. The wife is rude, the other doesn't give a fuck. It is only a moment and then I remember... The glasses and the knives and spoons engraved with the M.

KATHRYN: Nick will you listen... The Southside. There's noise coming from the Southside. It's okay...? You sent Makin? You sent fucking Makin?

GILMA comes back in.

GILMA: Who's fucking Makin?

KATHRYN: (*As loses signal.*) I'm stuck here and fucking Makin's on the fucking South – Fuck.

GENEVIEVE: Kathryn, my mother's name.

KATHRYN: I'm sorry. I don't understand.

GENEVIEVE: (*Gesturing.*) My mother? Katerina. It's actually the same name.

KATHRYN: Your mother? Right. It's common. I imagine the world over. My mother's was Margaret.

GENEVIEVE: Sorry. I don't understand.

GILMA: In a bin, by the window there's an old MacDonald's bag. Brown with the M – Millennium.

MICHELEINE: My grandson. Yesterday. He just loves MacDonald's.

GILMA: And *Toy Story*. On the table. Now in my coat.

A sound. A bang. Shelling. Fireworks. Something. Somewhere.

MICHELEINE: The windows are open. It feels very cold in here.

KATHRYN: Micheleine –

MICHELEINE: I'll close them.

KATHRYN: Ask her –

GILMA: Outside. Do you know what is going on outside?

GENEVIEVE: There must be a certain kind of –

GILMA: (*To KATHRYN.*) …professional ambition, she's asking –

GENEVIEVE: (*To KATHRYN.*) …I expect it's dangerous –

KATHRYN: (*Eyeing MICHELEINE.*) She's shaking…

MICHELEINE: I'm shaking. I can hardly close the window.

GENEVIEVE: …especially abroad. To be so eager to get your pictures in the papers.

MICHELEINE: If there's no wind, even the river sounds… sounds not far away.

KATHRYN: (*To GILMA.*) Tell her, I haven't really ever thought about it before.

MICHELEINE: But you've travelled here, a long way? That shows a certain passion, a certain belief to do, what you do?

KATHRYN: In the Northern states I took a photo…there is an old man. He is holding up a baby. The baby has no eyes. I suppose… Tell her, yes, I guess yes.

MICHELEINE: Gilma. (*Beat.*) You're not married yet?

GILMA: I'm waiting. For someone to come back.

MICHELEINE: A soldier?

GILMA: A soldier.

MICHELEINE: That's marvellous. That's marvellous.

GILMA: Before I was a lecturer, in science, in physical science. Before all this happened…

MICHELEINE: And look at you now.

GILMA: (*Beat.*) She patronises me.

MICHELEINE: I'm getting drunk.

That's clever. You are obviously very clever. You can't quite hear it… Your accent? Am I right?

GILMA: My accent?

MICHELEINE: Its Northern edge. You've softened it. Smoothed it over.

GILMA: I don't think so. I've been here a long time.

MICHELEINE: A long time. (*Beat.*) I mustn't have any more. (*Beat.*) I don't like to tell her but she has my *Toy Story* in her pocket.

KATHRYN holds up her bag to MICHELEINE.

KATHRYN: Is it okay, if I…? Gilma?

GILMA: Is it okay? To unpack her things?

MICHELEINE: Please tell her – (*Calling out.*) Marianna…
Will she need some help?

KATHRYN shakes her head. She begins to unpack her things.

(*Eyeing GILMA.*) I could possibly negotiate. Appeal to
her better nature. It is the favourite film of a very little
boy but –

GENEVIEVE: It's the view from our window. Not everyone
can see it. It's…

KATHRYN: Abstract.

GENEVIEVE: Exactly. Not everyone gets it. It was painted
by my husband when he was –

GILMA: (*To KATHRYN.*) …still alive. He was found… How
do you say?

MICHELEINE: Excuse me a moment.

GENEVIEVE: Tell her, he'd been depressed for a very long
time.

MICHELEINE: (*Calling out.*) Marianna. Marianna. We need
more ice.

*MICHELEINE walks across the room, ice bucket in hand
in search of some ice. She suddenly stands as if she is on the
telephone.*

(*Beat.*) Genevieve?

MICHELEINE: Genevieve, just listen for a moment, listen
and I will tell you as best I can.

KATHRYN: Somewhere, in a different house, in a different street not far away, this woman in her green dress is summoned to the phone.

MICHELEINE: Genevieve?

GENEVIEVE: Micheleine, you've caught me watching the television. That thing where –

MICHELEINE: Of course. Come over right now.

GENEVIEVE: …the man wins a million?

GILMA touches KATHRYN's camera equipment.

MICHELEINE: Don't be silly. That would be fine. Genie.

KATHRYN: It's clear, she's bluffing it…

GENEVIEVE: Micheleine, are you listening? Who are you talking to?

MICHELEINE: There's a lady from the press and we're having a few drinks. He's not back yet… Uh, you know how his work is?

KATHRYN puts out one hand to stop GILMA picking up a lens.

KATHRYN: Excuse me…

GILMA: Sorry.

KATHRYN: It's just the grease from your fingers. We all have it and don't know it. It smudges the lens.

GILMA: What's this?

KATHRYN: A light meter.

GILMA: What's it do?

KATHRYN: It measures light. It says the lights fading.

GILMA: She looks at her watch.

MICHELEINE: (*As if on the phone.*) You wouldn't be interrupting. We'd love you to come round…

GENEVIEVE: Micheleine and I have been friends for…

MICHELEINE: Twenty –

GENEVIEVE: …five –

MICHELEINE: …years… We believe in the same things. Our children…

GENEVIEVE: …don't get on.

'Micheleine, I'm in the middle of making supper… Micheleine…'

MICHELEINE: She's very lonely. Her husband…

GENEVIEVE: She's been very good to me. She's been very kind to me.

MICHELEINE: Sometimes I have to fight to get the time on my own. Sometimes she calls and I don't want to talk to her sometimes…but today…she's my very best friend.

❖

KATHRYN: Your husband was a painter?

GENEVIEVE: At the local art college…

MICHELEINE: Our husbands were school-friends, that's how we met. Tell them the story of the first time you visited…

GENEVIEVE: Micheleine…

MICHELEINE: A dinner party, the first we ever had…

GENEVIEVE: In that flat…

MICHELEINE: Above the butchers. We were so poor…

GENEVIEVE: Scrag end of lamb…

MICHELEINE: And after someone had brought a bottle of…

GENEVIEVE: Pie-eyed…

MICHELEINE: Pie-eyed…

GENEVIEVE: From some grass…

MICHELEINE: My father's place in the mountain… My brother and I used to…

GENEVIEVE: Dry it in their loft… And later… When most of the others had gone home…

MICHELEINE: We danced with each other because our…

GENEVIEVE: Preferred to talk…

MICHELEINE: They hated it most when we would giggle…

GENEVIEVE: …while they talked rubbish late into the night.

MICHELEINE: How can you say that?

GENEVIEVE: This is where we differ…

MICHELEINE: My husband never talked an ounce of rubbish in his life…

A ripple of laughter broken only by the smash of glass.

GILMA stands with pieces of the broken vase in her hand. A silence broken only by the ring of the phone. MICHELEINE lets it ring for some time until –

GILMA: I'm sorry. It was just… In my hand.

MICHELEINE: Venetian.

GILMA: I'm sorry.

MICHELEINE: I bought it with my husband, on an official visit abroad…

GENEVIEVE: A gift which she gave to our friend Isabella, a gift now returned to her.

MICHELEINE: 'But Isabella.'

> She silences me. This woman gives me back a vase, this woman does not want anything of us.

> Don't drink so much. Don't drink so much. Get a grip get a…

> I'll see if I can find Marianna. (*Calling out.*) Marianna. Marianna, excuse me please –

> *MICHELEINE goes as if to answer it.*

GILMA: Christ.

> *GILMA bends down to pick up the pieces of broken glass on the floor.*

MICHELEINE: (*As if on the phone.*) Hello… Hello…

> *MICHELEINE hangs up returning, bearing a dustpan and brush, handing it in passing to GILMA.*

❖

MICHELEINE: Genevieve –

> *GILMA bends down and starts to sweep up the broken vase as GENEVIEVE stands once more in familiar pose, pulling the scarf off from around her neck. The repetition is faster, now slightly more fragmented.*

GILMA: …hair dripping –

KATHRYN: …green dress.

GENEVIEVE: The roads are –

KATHRYN: …terrible.

MICHELEINE: Snow –

GENEVIEVE looking at GILMA as she sweeps up on the floor.

Just a bit of glass. (*As if introducing.*) Gilma.

GENEVIEVE: Gilma.

GENEVIEVE waves away MICHELEINE as she goes to take her coat.

Don't…

GILMA: …look me up and down like that.

GENEVIEVE: Micha… Micha… Is there anything to drink?

MICHELEINE: We're onto our third. How's Darius? And Marcus?

GENEVIEVE: He called only last week. He's going to bring…

GENEVIEVE walks across the room and pours herself a glass of vodka. The phone rings.

Jesus –

KATHRYN: Chilli vodka. In the house of an important man.

MICHELEINE: Lunch with Isabella.

GENEVIEVE: You saw her?

MICHELEINE: A few hours ago. (*Beat.*) You're freezing. What have you – ?

GENEVIEVE: …lying in the snow.

MICHELEINE: I'll get you… I'll get you… I'll get you a towel.

MICHELEINE exits in search of a towel. The phone stops ringing.

KATHRYN: This man that I've come to see, this man is a general, a man who is now on the edge of defeat. This man is a figure who fascinates, appallingly fascinates, this man, is now, too many hours late.

GILMA: (*To MICHELEINE.*) I'm sorry.

MICHELEINE: (*To GENEVIEVE.*) Sit down sit down. I hate it when you hover… We thought by the window. Sitting at his desk.

GENEVIEVE: Sorry… Sorry…

KATHRYN: He sends fucking Makin. Scandinavian. World Service. Blonde. Too blonde. With some work done to her lips.

They sit. A silence. Time ticks by.

GENEVIEVE: Well this…

KATHRYN: Yes…

GENEVIEVE: This is… Very exciting… (*To GILMA.*) She must visit our –

KATHRYN: Northern States. I cover mainly the Northern states.

GENEVIEVE: …coastal towns. It's very exciting to have a visitor from abroad…

MICHELEINE: Genie, don't embarrass yourself. You're gushing.

GENEVIEVE: You're drinking too much.

GENEVIEVE comes up to look at the painting with KATHRYN.

(*To KATHRYN.*) I see you've noticed the painting.

KATHRYN: Sorry?

GENEVIEVE: The painting? The painting on the wall?

KATHRYN: I'm sorry… (*To GILMA.*) Gilma?

GENEVIEVE: Does she like it? Can you ask her? What does she think of that painting?

KATHRYN looks directly at GENEVIEVE.

KATHRYN: When you go to countries where terrible things have happened, things that I cannot mention, things that I prefer to look at through the eye of a lens, when you go to these countries the thing that shocks you is that you are so shocked you are not shocked at all.

The phone rings.

MICHELEINE: (*Calling out.*) Marianna…

GENEVIEVE: My husband painted –

MICHELEINE: (*Beat.*) I forgot, today is her half day.

No one answers it.

KATHRYN: Then something throws you, some incongruous object, a child's rubber ring or a school book in the mud, or a grown man crying because he can't get a jar open, a jar of honey which he has found in the wreck of his house. You are touched for a moment by the horror of it all and you close the door quickly, you close it because you can't look…

GILMA: She wants to know what you think of the painting.

KATHRYN: That painting…that painting is the foot in the door.

A beat. The phone stops ringing.

GENEVIEVE: What did she say?

GILMA: Not much at all.

MICHELEINE: Someone will have answered it.

GILMA: (*To KATHRYN.*) Someone will have answered it.

KATHRYN: Gilma, I need to get over to the Southside.

MICHELEINE: (*Beat.*) My husband had he not joined the political arena may have been an architect…

GILMA: (*To KATHRYN.*) A builder…

KATHRYN: I'd like to use the phone?

MICHELEINE: (*Beat.*) My daughter. My grandson they live on the Southside.

GILMA: (*Holding up video.*) *A Bug's Life.* Second favourite after *Toy Story.*

KATHRYN: Cartoons. Fuck. Fuck.

GILMA: Could I watch?

MICHELEINE: If you'd like –

KATHRYN: No.

MICHELEINE: She's rude. So sharp. Why are you so rude? They're being rude to me.

Oolio, where are you? Sweetheart, where are you?

KATHRYN: She tells us the story of the first time she met him –

MICHELEINE: I was standing in the library. He kissed me on my neck. Have I told you this story?

GENEVIEVE: No darling, you've not told me.

KATHRYN: She has… Several times… It is clear on the woman's face.

GILMA: (*As if to KATHRYN.*) Her husband made love to her –

MICHELEINE: …around the great buildings of our city…

GILMA: (*As if to KATHRYN.*) Fish markets…and how do you say…the place where you…watch the sharks swim.

KATHRYN: Aquarium.

GILMA: Aquarium.

KATHRYN: How unusual…

GENEVIEVE: Yes…

GILMA: I guess yes.

MICHELEINE: (*To GILMA.*) I'm watching you.

GILMA: Amazing, how they get the bugs to talk like that –

MICHELEINE: She thinks that they're real. Christ –

GILMA: She thinks I think they're real. Christ –

GENEVIEVE: (*To GILMA.*) Kathryn, with your work? You must have travelled?

MICHELEINE: Genie, don't bother her –

KATHRYN: All the time she is talking –

MICHELEINE: …my husband always says busy people find it boring to discuss work.

KATHRYN: …her skin is pulling tighter across her mouth, and tiny specks of powder blot the beads of sweat around her nose. The light has now quite gone, I am resigned to lamplight and whatever I can find.

MICHELEINE: We thought by the window.

GENEVIEVE: Micheleine. It's nearly ten o'clock –

MICHELEINE: Please don't ask – Please don't ask again.

KATHRYN: …and we've been here since four.

GENEVIEVE: When Micheleine calls I am not watching the TV programme. The one where the man wins a million. I am sitting in my kitchen. I have turned all the lights off. It is dark and outside…the noise is lighting up the sky.

Somewhere there are people smashing shop windows.
And upstairs my neighbour has just hit his wife.

MICHELEINE: Genevieve?

GENEVIEVE: 'You've caught me watching the television.
That thing on the television?'

MICHELEINE: Of course. Why not come over?

GENEVIEVE: 'The one where the man wins a million?'

MICHELEINE: No, that would be fine. That would be
absolutely wonderful.

GENEVIEVE: 'Micheleine…'

MICHELEINE: (*Beat.*) There's a lady, she's here from
the press.

GENEVIEVE: I put down the phone and sit for several
minutes. Upstairs I can already hear someone moving
out. They are filling their car with as much as they can
carry. Knowing that their Northern neighbours may no
longer be their friends. I listen as they bump a washing
machine down the stairs. I wonder what I'll take.
Certainly not a washing machine and suddenly I realise
I'm not going anywhere.

'Micheleine, of course, of course I'll come over.' (*Beat.*)
Twenty –

MICHELEINE: … five –

GENEVIEVE: – years is a long time to despise your best
friend. (*To KATHRYN.*) Why do you look like that?

KATHRYN: Ask her, ask her how her husband died?

GILMA: (*To GENEVIEVE.*) Beautiful colours.

GENEVIEVE: Sorry?

GILMA: (*To GENEVIEVE.*) She thinks beautiful colours.

GENEVIEVE: That's not what she said.

KATHRYN: It's clear he's not coming.

MICHELEINE: I assure you. I assure you…

GENEVIEVE: Will you calm, Micheleine? Calm.

MICHELEINE: His ulcer is grumbling and he's waiting for some papers. There are some papers he said he has to sign.

GENEVIEVE: (*Beat.*) Feed them. It's suppertime. They're probably hungry.

GILMA: She says that she's starving.

MICHELEINE: (*Eyeing GILMA.*) It is you who is starving.

GILMA: There is fruit and some cheese and some left over cuts.

The sound of footsteps as though someone is walking down a long silent corridor.

MICHELEINE: I walk down the corridor to the ground floor kitchen. I notice that the lights have not been turned on in the west wing behind. The darkness is surprising, unfamiliar, unordered. It is ten and by ten, there should be every light on in the house. In the kitchen I still hope to find Marianna. (*Calling out.*) Marianna. (*Beat.*) She normally stays until we are all fed. The oven is off, the larder is empty, she has even taken the flour and sugar from the jars. (*Beat.*) I forget, it's her half day. I scrabble… I scrabble together some kind of supper… Some cheese, some oranges and there is some fat pork at the back of the fridge. I arrange them on a plate, as best I can. I walk back along the corridor. I see fires burning far away, lighting my route back.

(*Whispering.*) Oolio… Oolio…

KATHRYN: She calls out a pet name.

KATHRYN is suddenly standing as if in her path, making MICHELEINE jump, almost laugh, her phone in her hand.

I can't get a signal.

MICHELEINE: Christ… Christ… You made me jump.

GENEVIEVE: How old are you?

GILMA: Twenty-four. I know I look older.

GENEVIEVE: No…

GILMA: Yes, I do. I know this. You don't have to lie.

KATHRYN and MICHELEINE hover, as if one doesn't know if the other should cross their path.

KATHRYN: Can I try it in here? (*As if entering a room.*) Wow…

MICHELEINE: For state entertaining. For official visits.

KATHRYN: Oolio?

MICHELEINE: A pet name. I thought I heard him come back.

KATHRYN: Outside, Micheleine? You are aware of what's going on the Southside? My office says there are riots building up over there.

MICHELEINE turns and heads back as if with the others.

MICHELEINE: I am aware of the young Northern girl, Gilma as she wipes her plate with the skin of an orange, eating the peel to get the last of the grease.

GILMA: Jackie Collins? My God, I love Jackie Collins.

MICHELEINE: I am aware of my best friend, my dearest friend, Genevieve who is trying to make conversation, trying to make everything alright…

GILMA: Second shelf. Lady Boss… American Star is her best.

MICHELEINE: I am aware of something happening outside of here, I can hear the noise, I just chose to lie. My husband, he finds them relaxing. I prefer…

GILMA: Shakespeare. The complete works…

As GILMA licks the last of the food off the plate with her fingers.

MICHELEINE: Please mind the china. The plates are a set.

GILMA: (*Holding glass.*) Nice glasses.

MICHELEINE: Siberian.

KATHRYN: I can see one in your pocket. I'm not an idiot. Put it back.

MICHELEINE: Gilma has a boyfriend. A soldier.

GENEVIEVE: That's very nice.

KATHRYN picks a book off the shelf, puts it back.

KATHRYN: Lady Boss. Sometimes there are pockets of insight that one can't help but try and shoot.

GENEVIEVE: A soldier?

GILMA: The State Military.

GENEVIEVE: That's admirable. A soldier –

MICHELEINE: Gilma's from the North.

A long silence.

KATHRYN: Your phone, may I use it?

GILMA: Where is your telephone please?

KATHRYN: Mine can't get a signal.

MICHELEINE: Left. Then right. Then left again.

KATHRYN goes to use the phone.

GILMA: The woman in the green dress watches me while I finish my food up. It is obvious what she is thinking. 'Her manners? Of course she's from the North.' I eat the orange peel not because I have to, not because I am in poverty but because I like the taste.

KATHRYN: I get through to the office. The line is faint.

GENEVIEVE: Your accent?

GILMA: It's been five years.

GENEVIEVE: You've visited your family?

GILMA: No. Not often.

GENEVIEVE: That's a pity. I couldn't live, I really couldn't without mine.

MICHELEINE: Liar.

They've never actually visited her. I love Genevieve. She's my very, very best friend but sometimes… I won't say this until we are alone.

GENEVIEVE: I'm sorry.

GILMA: Sorry? What is there to be sorry about?

KATHRYN: (*As if on phone.*) Nick… Nick… Which bridge? Which bridge? I can't walk… It's freezing… Are you going to get me a taxi…? Nick. It's not happening… It's just not happening. We've been here since four, because the light has gone.

GILMA: I visit my family, one day last summer. They ask me how I am. I can't bear the way they eat. I show them the clothes and the things that I have brought them. A jacket from Marks and Spencer's. A video – a hip and thigh diet for my mother. 'Hip and thigh…hip and thigh…where is the food for me to get fat?' This is said, so that I send more money for them each month. 'Even in a war you must make the effort… Even in a war, mother…' Even in a war, I polish my shoes.

MICHELEINE: Gilma has a boyfriend. A soldier.

GENEVIEVE: That's very nice. A soldier? I hope you love him very, very much.

MICHELEINE: You –

GILMA: …plan to get married when he gets home.

As soon as I say this, I wish that I hadn't. Not because I am lying but because it was never true.

KATHRYN: (*As if on the phone.*) …I don't know what's going on here. I don't know why I'm here. Nick, don't piss around. I don't know what to do now. You sent Makin.

GILMA: Fucking, fucking Makin.

KATHRYN: (*As if on the phone.*) Fuck you. Fuck you. Yeah fuck her too.

GILMA: She swears a lot. (*Beat.*) Her office is telling her to stay where she is.

KATHRYN: (*As if on the phone.*) He may have asked for me but he's not fucking here.

KATHRYN, as if slamming down the phone.

Gilma, the taxi. We can we get the taxi?

GILMA: We said not until later. We have to wait.

MICHELEINE: My husband has a driver. Perhaps I could call him.

GILMA: She makes gestures to find her diary and call her husband at work.

GENEVIEVE: Your work must be fascinating you take photos for a living?

MICHELEINE: Genie, don't bother her. Oolio says busy people don't like talking about work.

KATHRYN: In places of crisis –

MICHELEINE: My favourite of us is at Christmas…

KATHRYN: …places of war.

GENEVIEVE: And you're not frightened? You're not moved by the things that you see?

KATHRYN: I'm sorry? I'm sorry?

GENEVIEVE: You don't understand at all.

MICHELEINE: It was taken last year. Christmas. With all of us. The family.

GENEVIEVE: Micha, have you called Angelica? Is she at home with the boy?

MICHELEINE goes and pours herself another drink.

KATHRYN: On the desk is a photo. Of her husband with his family. He is wearing a paper hat, he is flushed, the hat's awry, like a comical drunkard or a man with one eye. There is a smile on his face and clasped around wrinkled fingers are those of his grandchild hugging the skin… He's very…

MICHELEINE: Like his grandfather… Do you have children?

KATHRYN: No. Not at all.

MICHELEINE: (*To KATHRYN.*) Are you married?

GILMA: She's asking if you are…

KATHRYN: No.

GENEVIEVE: I imagine there is no time…no time with your work…

KATHRYN: Sometimes it is easier if I say I am married. Sometimes it is easier…

MICHELEINE: *Bug's Life*. Now also stolen. Slipped in her jacket. *Toy Story* in her pocket. *Bug's Life* most probably wedged under her bra.

This portrait of my husband? This portrait that you plan to take? You must be important. He rarely courts press.

KATHRYN: It was agreed through my office. A request from his advisors.

MICHELEINE: He's a man you admire?

KATHRYN: More fascinated.

GILMA: More fascinated.

MICHELEINE: To me he's my husband.

KATHRYN: And to the rest of the world?

The phone rings. And rings until – it stops.

GILMA: …You drove along the…

GENEVIEVE: Past the Gymnasium…

GILMA: As a child I used to swim there. I taught there for two semesters. Before they… I was there the day they filled in the pool.

MICHELEINE: The changing rooms are now offices and the athletic pitch barracks… We needed headquarters. (*Beat.*) I suggested it one evening after supper in bed.

GENEVIEVE: She wants us to admire her.

KATHRYN: In this light she is almost bearable.

MICHELEINE: By morning there were engineers knocking down walls.

GILMA: Your husband used to go there?

MICHELEINE: He'd been depressed a long time.

GENEVIEVE: With my children.

MICHELEINE: Don't upset her.

GENEVIEVE: Marcus is twenty-one. Darius our youngest is almost eighteen.

MICHELEINE: You've heard from him?

GENEVIEVE: Last week. A painter like his father. He's been skiing for the winter.

MICHELEINE: She is lying.

KATHRYN: She is lying.

GENEVIEVE: He's met a new girl. He doesn't say exactly but as a mother you know.

MICHELEINE: Genevieve.

KATHRYN: The look on her face says she is desperate for us to believe her. The look on her face knows we suspect it's not true.

MICHELEINE: (*Beat.*) A girlfriend. At last. We had money on it he was…

GENEVIEVE: My husband used to tease him. He is gentle like his father. (*To GILMA.*) You don't have children?

GILMA: No. Not yet…

GENEVIEVE: And you?

KATHRYN: No, not at all.

MICHELEINE: (*To GENEVIEVE.*) It's a joke. Don't look so serious. You take me far too seriously.

KATHRYN: (*Watching GILMA and GENEVIEVE.*) She offers her an orange. The woman in the green dress.

The phone rings. MICHELEINE eventually gets up to answer it.

MICHELEINE: Hello. (*Long silence.*) Don't do that darling. (*Breaking into a long broad smile.*) He's teasing me on the telephone… We're eating… Only cold cuts… (*Calling out.*) We'll leave some for you.

GENEVIEVE: As we drink the last of the vodka, her comment still burns me. You may have had money on it Micha, but I know my son is not gay.

MICHELEINE: All the time that I am talking they shell oranges on my floor.

KATHRYN: All the time that the wife is talking, the lady in the green dress is pulling a thread from the corner of her skirt.

GILMA: It's lovely… It's lovely… That green is a lovely colour…

GENEVIEVE: You think so?

GILMA: I think so…

MICHELEINE laughs, still on the telephone.

(*Eyeing GENEVIEVE.*) She has five notes in her purse. A bus ticket and a library card. And a photo of a man, he is eating a hunk of sausage and standing with a watering can, squinting in the sun.

GENEVIEVE: My husband was fascinated with light and how it fell on life… His paintings were also the balance of dark and light…

KATHRYN: You're crying.

GENEVIEVE gets up to pour herself another drink.

You're crying. You're trying not to show us. But as you pour yourself a drink, there are tears in your eyes.

GILMA touching KATHRYN's camera equipment.

KATHRYN: (*To GILMA.*) Don't do that… Please don't do that… You keep on touching…

GILMA: Sorry…

KATHRYN: If you keep on touching you'll get grease on the lens.

MICHELEINE enters as if off the phone.

MICHELEINE: He asks that you leave him some of the ham, please. It's his favourite, his sister sends it from her own farm.

She stares at me. I turn and catch her eye, aware she's always watching me.

KATHRYN: You don't look…

MICHELEINE: Forty-five, forty-six next month.

KATHRYN: She's a vain woman. This flatters her.

GILMA: She says you don't look it… She says…

KATHRYN: Tell her she has beautiful skin.

MICHELEINE: That's really very nice of you… That's really very kind of you…

GILMA: I take the five notes and a photograph.

MICHELEINE walks across the room, takes a packet of cigarette, lights one.

I slip the purse of the green lady back in her bag.

GENEVIEVE: In my house I have several photos. Of Micheleine with my family. Micheleine and him and my husband and me. On boating trips and birthdays and there is even one at my husband's memorial. Micheleine sitting, head bent down at her husband's side.

KATHRYN: She has this way of turning her head, as if trained, as if knowing that this is captivating…

GENEVIEVE: The photo was commented upon, noted, that they both visibly cried.

(*To anyone.*) I have the most marvellous photo of Micheleine at my home.

MICHELEINE: There's an edge in her voice.

GILMA: She says she has a photograph of Micheleine at her husband's funeral.

KATHRYN: She barely can look at us. She can barely believe she's said it.

MICHELEINE: Have you, Genie? I don't think I've seen that one.

GENEVIEVE: I always admired the coat you wore.

MICHELEINE: You can borrow it…

GILMA scoops the vase up in her hand, holds it.

KATHRYN: I don't need to understand to understand.

MICHELEINE: …any time at all.

GILMA stands listening as the vase breaks. A silence broken only by the ring of the phone. MICHELEINE lets it ring for some time until –

GILMA: I'm so sorry. It was just… In my hand.

MICHELEINE: (*Calling out.*) Marianna… Marianna… I'll get you. (*Calling out.*) Marianna… I get you… I'll one minute… (*Going.*) We need more ice.

MICHELEINE scoops up the ice bucket to go and get more ice. The phone stops ringing.

GENEVIEVE: I climb into the car and bolt the gate behind me. My neighbour has many possessions littered across the grass. A washing machine, a wheelbarrow, a bed, a table… 'You should think of leaving. They won't want you staying here.' I chose to ignore him. I'm not ungracious. I'm not unfriendly. As I pass in the car, I see his dog sleeping in the machine's metal drum. I drive along North route and past the Gymnasium.

I stop. I lie in the snow too long. I think of going to sleep.

After, the streets are already littered and there are several broken panes of glass. Someone has set off a burglar alarm and there is a crowd near the crossroads. I lean forward and lock my doors. I take the back route here. I drive through the gates and already I know it is over. Maybe now my sons can come back.

MICHELEINE enters, back with a fresh ice bucket of ice, passing the dustpan and brush to GILMA.

MICHELEINE: Genevieve –

MICHELEINE stands. GILMA is once more on the floor sweeping up some glass with a dustpan and brush. KATHRYN is standing looking at the painting. GENEVIEVE now has her coat on, her hair still wet, pulling off her scarf as if she has just arrived. The repetition is faster, fragmented into a ricochet of words.

Hair…

GENEVIEVE: Snow

GILMA sweeps up on the floor.

MICHELEINE: Venetian… Special vase –

GENEVIEVE: The roads…

KATHRYN: Green dress.

GENEVIEVE: Oolio –

MICHELEINE offers KATHRYN a cigarette. KATHRYN declines. GENEVIEVE pours herself a glass of vodka.

MICHELEINE: Onto our third.

The phone rings.

Genevieve. Kathryn… Gilma… Best to go through her. You're freezing…

GENEVIEVE: The heater on my car packed up…

KATHRYN: You have a car?

GENEVIEVE: Very old. Very battered.

MICHELEINE: I am shaking. I am frightened. I want to tell them I am very, very frightened. I had not planned for this. What happens next?

GENEVIEVE: Micheleine, there is trouble –

MICHELEINE: I was telling them how we first met.

GENEVIEVE: As far as the North route.

MICHELEINE: The military?

GENEVIEVE: Are not around.

MICHELEINE: Hair…

GENEVIEVE: …dripping.

MICHELEINE: Towel…

MICHELEINE goes to get GENEVIEVE a towel. GENEVIEVE watches KATHRYN looking at the painting. The phone stops ringing.

GENEVIEVE: (*To KATHRYN.*) The view from our window… From our house… You see? That is the river and that is the persons…

KATHRYN: And which bit are people?

GENEVIEVE: You see their faces?

KATHRYN: Your husband painted?

Your husband painted it?

For them?

GENEVIEVE nods.

GENEVIEVE: (*To GILMA.*) Tell her, will you tell her, I find it frightening too.

MICHELEINE enters and drops the towel into GENEVIEVE's lap.

GILMA: They are talking about the painting. All three standing in front of it. That is when I take *A Bug's Life*. That is when. When their backs are all turned. Earlier Kathryn has asked her –

A sound. A bang. Shelling. Fireworks. Something. Somewhere.

KATHRYN: The noise?

MICHELEINE: It's much louder if you have the windows open.

GILMA: She closes them. Ignores our gaze. I translate of course.

MICHELEINE: On a clear day…

GILMA: When there's no wind…

MICHELEINE: You can hear almost everything. The silence carries everything.

GENEVIEVE: When the children were younger you could sometimes hear them splashing no matter how far you were from the swimming pool.

MICHELEINE takes the towel, rubs GENEVIEVE's hair.

MICHELEINE: Genevieve. Don't gush now. What are we to do with you?

GENEVIEVE hands back the towel to MICHELEINE.

Help me, Genie, help me. I don't know what to do.

GILMA: (*Watching MICHELEINE.*) She's frightened. You can see this. She smiles but she is frightened. Her mind is elsewhere. She won't notice what I take.

MICHELEINE: When I pick up the phone, the first time there is no one. The silence is empty but there is definitely someone there… The second time I can hear them talking in the other room…

GENEVIEVE: My husband was fascinated with light and how it fell on life…

MICHELEINE: She's trying to impress them, flaying around in artist talk…

'Hello.' (*Long silence.*) 'Don't do that darling.'

Someone is sending insults down the line… Terrible words cutting through the silence –

'Bitch. Whore. This is the end.'

A Northern accent. (*Breaking into a long broad smile.*) He's teasing me on the telephone.

KATHRYN: Most times when you are working there is no time to set your photo. You don't want to, you shoot it just as you see…

A sound. A bang. Shelling. Fireworks. Something. Somewhere.

GILMA: Bang.

A ripple of laughter as GILMA makes them laugh.

MICHELEINE: A noise. Like gun fire.

I am worried because I think I hear a young boy crying. I am worried because…

Beat.

My daughter… Angeli…lives on the Southside.

KATHRYN: If you keep on touching you'll get grease on the lens.

MICHELEINE, as if re-entering the room.

MICHELEINE: He asks that you leave him some of the ham, please. It's his favourite, his sister sends it from her own farm.

GENEVIEVE: Micheleine…

MICHELEINE: It wasn't him… It was someone… I don't know who it was… It was someone…

GENEVIEVE: How did they get your number?

MICHELEINE: I don't know… I don't know…

GILMA: If I hadn't been a lecturer, I might have been a photographer…

KATHRYN: People always say that…

GILMA: Do they? I wonder why.

GENEVIEVE: Call him.

MICHELEINE: I have tried. I don't even get his secretary.

GENEVIEVE: Do you think?

MICHELEINE: No.

GENEVIEVE: Do you think maybe…

MICHELEINE: No.

GILMA: Buzz Lightyear is not real, he's an electronic space man and the cowboy…he's the hero. He doesn't like it when he moves in on his patch.

MICHELEINE: What are they talking about?

GENEVIEVE: They're making conversation.

GILMA: The cowboy is in love with… I can't remember who the girl is.

KATHRYN: Barbie?

GILMA: Of course, Barbie, but she is the fantasy, the cowboy has a real love that the space man steals.

KATHRYN: This is a ridiculous conversation… This is a fucking ridiculous conversation…

MICHELEINE: Bo Peep. It's Bo Peep. I've watched it with my grandson.

GILMA: Of course it all turns out alright in the end.

KATHRYN: The wife is upset. She is being hushed by the woman in the green dress. (*To GENEVIEVE.*) You're freezing…

GENEVIEVE: The heater on my…

KATHRYN: Could you drive me, if I paid you, over to the Southside?

GILMA: On the Southside is the flat where I live with my boyfriend's mother. She is poor and I work to make sure there is money coming in –

GENEVIEVE: The North route is log jammed…

KATHRYN: But there's a road, we drove past it…

GENEVIEVE: I can't.

KATHRYN: Please –

GENEVIEVE: Don't ask me. I can't.

MICHELEINE: She can't. Alright? Alright.

Beat.

GILMA: This morning I receive a call from my agency. There is one phone in the hall, which you can only use at certain times in the day. I am told I am to come to interpret for the wife of a diplomat and a journalist, a photographer who is coming into town. Giving the taxi driver instructions which I have picked up from the agency, it is only then I realise where it is we are to go. He is not just a diplomat, he is more than a diplomat. My mother-in-law is excited.

MICHELEINE: Gilma's from the North.

GILMA: I decide not to lie.

GENEVIEVE: Your accent?

GILMA: It's been five years.

GENEVIEVE: You've visited your family?

GILMA: Sometimes.

GENEVIEVE: (*To KATHRYN.*) I'm sorry. I can't. The roads are too icy.

KATHRYN: Snow.

GILMA: Snow, slowly falling outside.

The four women stand as if looking out of the window, watching the snow fall as it floats by outside.

GENEVIEVE: The night my husband died –

MICHELEINE: You were having supper with us…

GENEVIEVE: He had gone to take the children to the Gym –

MICHELEINE: And left her all alone. I persuaded you to come and eat with us… Our husbands were school friends, that's how we met. Tell them the story of the first time you visited…

GENEVIEVE: Micheleine…

MICHELEINE: A dinner party, the first we ever had…

GENEVIEVE: In that flat…

MICHELEINE: Above the butchers…

GENEVIEVE: Pie-eyed…

MICHELEINE: Preferred to dance…

GENEVIEVE: …while they talked rubbish late into the night…

MICHELEINE: This is where we differ… My husband never talked an ounce of rubbish in his life…

GENEVIEVE gets up and goes to look out of the window.

KATHRYN: Maybe if I could take the car. I have an international driver's licence.

MICHELEINE: And insurance? You have the right kind of insurance? I didn't think so. That would be dangerous.

KATHRYN: In times like these –

MICHELEINE: Have you no family? Someone you should think of. Have you no one who may be worried about you back home.

GENEVIEVE: I don't think it would get you there.

KATHRYN: It is no more dangerous than what is going on in here. Translate it… Gilma will you please tell her what I said?

GILMA: The car's fucked. Don't keep asking. I've paid for the taxi. To take us back to the Southside.

KATHRYN looks to GILMA who remains silent until –

She says that is fine. She will wait for the taxi ride.

MICHELEINE nods offers KATHRYN another orange from the bowl… KATHRYN hesitates then takes it and starts to peel, she walks as if going outside.

GENEVIEVE: Fireworks.

KATHRYN nods. They look up as if above the sky has just lit up.

KATHRYN: Fireworks. And not even November…

GENEVIEVE: Sorry…

KATHRYN: It doesn't matter.

GENEVIEVE: I'm sorry. I don't understand.

KATHRYN: Sometimes, tonight, I wonder why I do this.

GENEVIEVE: I loved my husband.

KATHRYN: Sorry?

GENEVIEVE: Love. I loved my husband.

KATHRYN: I'm sorry? I don't know what you're saying.

GENEVIEVE: I want you to know that.

KATHRYN: I don't know…

I'm sorry.

GENEVIEVE: You don't need to understand to understand.

GILMA peels an orange.

MICHELEINE: There's a bowl…

GILMA: She is watching even when I peel an orange.

MICHELEINE: Why don't you put your peel in the bowl?

GILMA: Sorry. Sorry.

MICHELEINE: There's no need to be sorry… (*Beat.*) Your boyfriend, the soldier, is he from the North?

GILMA: His family live here, here in the city.

MICHELEINE: I thought not. I thought not in the army. If he was from the North, they wouldn't let him in.

GILMA pauses in peeling her orange, letting the peel drop to the floor.

KATHRYN: How far away? (*Beat.*) The noise? The light? I was wondering how far it was actually away? It's getting nearer.

GENEVIEVE: (*Looking at KATHRYN.*) I wonder, looking at this woman, if this was a different time, if we spoke the same language, if this hadn't happened, if I wasn't me and this all hadn't happened, would we be friends?

KATHRYN: The light. It doesn't matter…

GENEVIEVE: She carries a kind of melancholia… Your family?

KATHRYN: Family. Just me. Not really any family.

GILMA: What are you fucking looking at?

GENEVIEVE: A kind of melancholia that is familiar to me.

MICHELEINE: *Bug's Life* in your coat. Don't think I haven't noticed, Gilma.

GILMA: Shit she's going to say it.

MICHELEINE: Gilma (*Long silence.*) you've some orange in your teeth.

GILMA picks, nods. Silence.

GILMA: Your husband is a great man.

MICHELEINE: To me he is my husband.

GILMA: My boyfriend has his picture above our bed.

MICHELEINE: He's a soldier. As it should be.

GILMA: Yes of course, as it should be –

MICHELEINE holds out her hand. GILMA disposes the peel into her hand.

Thank you.

MICHELEINE: You're welcome. Gilma.

GILMA: Gilma. Micheleine.

KATHRYN: The woman in the green dress is shivering… Genevieve?

GENEVIEVE: Genevieve.

KATHRYN: You're shivering… We can go inside.

GILMA flicks through one of the books on the shelf.

GILMA: Are you not worried about your husband?

MICHELEINE: Are you not worried about your soldier?

GENEVIEVE puts out a hand as if stopping KATHRYN.

GENEVIEVE: Kathryn?

KATHRYN: Kathryn. She puts out her arm. Stops me.

GENEVIEVE: Kathryn.

KATHRYN: Holds me with her look.

GENEVIEVE: Don't be like me.

KATHRYN: What are you saying?

GENEVIEVE: I lay in the snow tonight and I wanted to sleep.

KATHRYN: I'm trying to understand what you are saying.

GENEVIEVE: Don't go. I have to tell you…

MICHELEINE rolls back laughing as if GILMA has just told her the funniest joke.

MICHELEINE: (*As if bursting into conversation.*) That is the rudest joke that I ever heard.

GILMA: He learned it in the army.

MICHELEINE: And it best stay there. We thought that you had gone…

GENEVIEVE: I was showing her the car.

KATHRYN: She's right, I can't drive it.

GILMA: The car is fucked.

KATHRYN: That's not what I said.

GILMA: She says you're right, she can't drive it. But thanks very much.

KATHRYN: If you are going to talk for me can you try and get it right.

GILMA: If you don't speak it how do you know what I am saying?

The phone rings. MICHELEINE does not move.

If you don't speak it how do you know what I am saying?

KATHRYN: I know.

GILMA: Pardon. (*Beat.*) You don't speak a word.

KATHRYN: Tell her I'm concerned her husband isn't coming, tell her…

The phone rings some more. GENEVIEVE goes and answers it.

GENEVIEVE: (*As if on the phone.*) At last... This isn't good
enough... You have us all waiting... I'll tell her but she
won't like it... (*Calling out.*) At least another hour... (*As
if into the phone.*) Yeah, yeah, yeah... This isn't your wife
you're talking to... (*Laughing.*) You listen, that kind of
talk doesn't wash with me...

GENEVIEVE, as if coming back off the phone.

That man I tell you is such a trickster, Micheleine, he
tried to seduce me right under your nose... He promises
kisses and sends his apologies. Less than an hour. (*To
KATHRYN.*) Thirty minutes at the most.

MICHELEINE: You spoke to him. He's on his way, Genie –

GENEVIEVE: Yes, I spoke to him. Apparently the papers
have only just arrived, he'll be here as soon as he's signed.

MICHELEINE: Did he give you a message? Did he not
want to speak to me?

GENEVIEVE: No.

MICHELEINE: No?

GENEVIEVE: No.

Is there any more to drink?

The photograph. Where did you find it? In your hand?
The photograph?

GILMA: Under your chair. It must have slipped...

GENEVIEVE: Out of my bag. Marcus is twenty-one.
Darius almost eighteen. There's a new girl. He doesn't
say exactly but I know –

MICHELEINE: (*Beat.*) A girlfriend. At last. We had money
on it he was...

GENEVIEVE: Gay. You're going to say he is gay. No. You always say that but no you are wrong.

MICHELEINE: What do I say? Genevieve, if I have upset you…

GENEVIEVE: You haven't but let us now at last set the record straight. My son is not gay. My son is gentle. My son is like his father, but for you it is easier to say…

MICHELEINE: Genie –

GENEVIEVE: Easier to say…

GILMA stands up and moves across the room, placing back the video of 'Toy Story' onto the table.

GILMA: My favourite is *Bug's Life* –

KATHRYN: She places it on the table. She is totally unashamed. The wife and the woman, the lady in the green dress, stop their arguing, the wife is momentarily bemused…

MICHELEINE: My grandson's.

GILMA: And there it is back. (*To MICHELEINE.*) Your husband is a man I admire, Miss. Your husband is a man who I believe is doing good. Your husband, I am grateful to your husband for all he has done –

MICHELEINE: For your people? For your family?

GILMA: My family is not my family. My family is my soldier. My family, like your husband, despises people from the North.

My mother says 'A soldier? You are sleeping with a soldier?' 'Yes, mother. Yes, mother. What is wrong with that?'

One day through her door my mother gets a tongue, cut out from the throat of my brother, her youngest son.

MICHELEINE: That's most surprising. I'll tell my husband. He will be surprised to find that…you…feel the same way. Well done.

GILMA: Bloody and dirty and staining the newspaper it's wrapped in. A dirty Northern tongue. A warning to us all.

You're welcome.

MICHELEINE: That's quite alright.

GILMA: What?

KATHRYN: In a Northern town not far away, an old man brings me a baby, a baby that the soldiers have gouged the eyes out from.

GILMA: What?

KATHRYN: The old man is holding the baby up to me to witness, holding it up, asking me to take it, to take it in some way.

GILMA: What?

KATHRYN: I feel sick. I feel sick, not because I have not seen this before, because I have just used the last of my film. I pretend to this man. I shoot anyway.

You're from the North.

GILMA: I'm whatever I want to be. In my pocket, is your licence. International. EEC. (*As if reading.*) Kathryn Margaret Foxton. Kate Foxton.

KATHRYN: Give that back.

GILMA: It fell out in the taxi. You might need it when you get home.

KATHRYN: I'm going to tell the agency. Not to use you again.

GILMA: That is fine. That is fine. I can always find work elsewhere.

KATHRYN: And after. Where do you go then? When your soldier is back? What happens then?

A sound. A bang. Shelling. Fireworks. Something. Faint. Yet closer than before.

KATHRYN: Did you hear that? What's happening?

GILMA: Sssh… The snow is blanketing the noise.

KATHRYN: (*Watching MICHELEINE.*) Lamplight. A window. The back of… She leans out… Her feet hang. Her nose pressed. Hard against the glass. The sound of… Somewhere… The snow keeps falling.

MICHELEINE: When I first met my husband, my father did not want us to marry, it was all a secret, I used to meet him at an old school hall outside of the town. One winter, when the snow was so thick that for days we would never leave the house, only my father would be picked up and driven to work. The days were very boring and my sister was so irritating and all I wanted to do was see him, this boy, who I did not yet know whether I loved, when there was a tap at the window and I looked down and it was him and I say… 'Ssh my little sister will give us away.' 'Don't worry my darling, no one will know that you have been with me, walk in my shoe steps, follow behind me and then there will be only one set of footprints in the snow.' So I followed him through the dark of a very, very short day and that afternoon, while my sister played house with my mother, we made love for the first time until I was sore –

He leans back to kiss me. A small patch of stubble. Something about his manner. Back in one hour.

I feel sick.

Genie, I'm rambling –

GENEVIEVE: It's late…

MICHELEINE: Did someone win a million – ?

GENEVIEVE: No, a fat lady had trouble with a question on the pope.

MICHELEINE: Did you know the answer?

GENEVIEVE: No.

MICHELEINE: You must read more, Genie, you really must read more.

A beat.

GENEVIEVE: New handbag.

MICHELEINE: Last season's.

GENEVIEVE: It doesn't look it.

MICHELEINE: You're sniping…

GENEVIEVE: I'm not, Sweetheart.

MICHELEINE: You're picking a fight.

GENEVIEVE: Micha, when I drove over, I saw they had firebombed the Southside.

MICHELEINE: Along the Terra –

GENEVIEVE: Yes –

MICHELEINE: Oh my God…my God…

KATHRYN: If I told you how many people were covering this catastrophe, if I told you how many people were probably over on the Southside…

GILMA: What do you want me to do about it?

What do you want me to do about it?

You're here now. You have to make the best of where you are.

Fuck Makin.

KATHRYN: Scandinavian. Working for the World Service press. National Geographic… Definitely, most definitely has had work done to her lips.

GILMA: You've not had sex, it's clear –

KATHRYN: Piss off.

GILMA: …in a very, very long time.

KATHRYN: Is swearing not universal?

GILMA: Desperate.

KATHRYN: Fuck you. Is that nice and clear?

GILMA: When? One year…two…

KATHRYN: Three… Three months ago…

GILMA: Not bad. And you enjoyed it?

KATHRYN: Laughing. Teeth rotten. Orange caught in her gums.

Yes I enjoyed it.

GILMA: (*Sniff.*) I sometimes get it wrong.

KATHRYN: Brief. Necessary. Uncomplicated. Uncommitted. Men like me. There's not a problem. Men like me for that.

GENEVIEVE comes through holding a coffee tray.

GENEVIEVE: I'm afraid there's no milk but (*Holding up a bar of chocolate.*) I found this treat.

KATHRYN: Thank you… Thank you…

GILMA: Is Micheleine alright?

GENEVIEVE: Her daughter she lives –

KATHRYN: With the boy?

GILMA: With the boy…

KATHRYN: Your family?

GILMA: …your family?

GENEVIEVE: …moved away when their father –

MICHELEINE: (*As if on the phone.*) As I ring the office…

The woman who finally answers is my husband's secretary. She spent last Christmas here when her house was burgled and she had nowhere to go.

'Where's Oolio…? He's not there? But he was coming to sign papers. He was coming to you to sign papers. But he's taken the car… There's noise. A lot of noise.'

The woman hangs up on MICHELEINE or is cut off. MICHELEINE takes the cup of coffee proffered in GENEVIEVE's hand and drinks.

See, he's on his way.

(*Aside to GENEVIEVE.*) He didn't call. You didn't talk to him –

GENEVIEVE: Micha –

MICHELEINE: Why did you lie?

GENEVIEVE: Did you want me to tell you that some man with a thick Northern voice, a thick Northern gruff voice, a thick angry Northern gruff voice thinks you're a whore?

I thought not. (*Beat.*) I thought not.

MICHELEINE: It's the waiting.

GENEVIEVE: Yes… I know… I understand that.

MICHELEINE suddenly breaks into a low, wailing, engulfing outpouring that shocks and silences those around her, for several seconds until, regaining composure –

MICHELEINE: No milk? The milk is on the sill. I put it there this morning. Excuse me…

KATHRYN: No one says anything until –

The clitter-clatter of heels as if disappearing down a long corridor.

MICHELEINE: I have never noticed until this day what a clitter-clatter my tiny mules make along this corridor. I have never noticed the way my husband winces every time I run to greet him, fuss around him, scoop the work papers out of his arms and ask him to tell me about his day. 'Darling, your shoes.' I thought it was just him…just his grumbling ulcer… I thought that my conversation… my concern…my direction when yet another problem fell in his lap, yet another blot on the landscape threatened to disrupt some important advance, soothed this noise. That my advice, taken, relied upon, needed, often acted upon, was enough to disguise the clitter-clatter of heels I have observed in other women.

'Where's Oolio?'

'He's not here'

'But he was coming to sign papers. He was coming to you to sign papers.'

'Micheleine, you must get out of the house. Micheleine you must get a car and get out of the house and get out of the city as soon as you can.'

'But he's taken the car…'

There's noise. A lot of noise…

'Micheleine. I can't talk to you now. He has left you. He has left us.'

The footsteps stop. MICHELEINE takes the milk and pours it into a jug.

KATHRYN: He wasn't on the phone, was he?

GENEVIEVE: No.

KATHRYN: If he has been… If he's left…

GENEVIEVE: I am sorry… I am sorry that you have come all this way… I am sorry –

KATHRYN: What are you sorry –

GENEVIEVE: …That you have walked into this mess…

KATHRYN: It's my job. This is what I do.

GILMA: Where's he gone?

GENEVIEVE: I don't know.

GILMA: At that moment I see my mother-in-law… My non-mother-in-law, my boyfriend's mother, where I live until my boyfriend comes home…

I kiss him with my dirty Northern tongue.

GILMA picks up the vase, once more lying on its side in newspaper.

Above his bed is a picture of the general, the husband. At that moment I see my mother-in-law screaming at others to get out. They have stolen her television and are writing things on the wall… The Northern invasion… It is with my mother-in-law that I have learnt to speak. She turns a blind out to the odd clumsy vowel, I assure her that this is a throwback to some distant relative a long time ago who came from the North side… I know she doesn't believe me but the money I bring in is more important to her. It is I who stole the trainers that she wears on her feet. Nike Air, size seven. Men's. Too big. Uncomfortable. Taken from a journalist who was careless with his bag. If this is it…if this has not been for anything better than this –

GILMA breaks the vase, looking up as MICHELEINE comes in bearing a dustpan and brush, a jug of milk in the other hand.

MICHELEINE: Gen…

GILMA bends down and starts to sweep up the broken vase as GENEVIEVE stands once more in familiar pose, pulling the scarf off from around her neck. Language is almost obliterated, the physical actions more important than what is said.

Hair…

KATHRYN: …Dripping…

GENEVIEVE: Kathryn…

GENEVIEVE and KATHRYN go to shake hands but stop.

KATHRYN: Tell her. Sounds outside. Woman in the green dress… Staring at me… Holding up a baby… Baby crying without any eyes…

Gilma, outside, ask her does she know that outside, the crowd, they'll be seeking a revenge.

MICHELEINE: A number is not important. A number is redundant. What means everything to one person and nothing to someone else.

GILMA does not respond.

KATHRYN: Gilma?

GILMA: I can't translate that.

MICHELEINE: (*To GENEVIEVE.*) I've been showing them my handbags.

KATHRYN: You won't translate that?

GILMA: I won't translate that.

GENEVIEVE: I think she is questioning whether it is right to stay.

MICHELEINE: (*To GENEVIEVE.*) Did you go? You did not. Even when your husband died. You did not leave. Did you? Did you? Look at your hair.

GENEVIEVE: Why have you stopped crying? I could feel sympathy for you when you were crying. I can remember the warmth of that night when we ate scrag end of lamb and our husbands danced with us and mocked us and laughed at us. And twenty-five years on here we are now.

I think she is right. I think you should go.

MICHELEINE: I'm not listening.

GENEVIEVE: You can hear me.

MICHELEINE: I'm just not listening.

GENEVIEVE: Oolio has left you…

MICHELEINE: (*Eyeing KATHRYN.*) You've been listening too much to her.

GENEVIEVE: On the way here, on the North route I passed the Terra Strata, the road is firebombed, my neighbours were cheering…

GILMA: The Terra Strata. My boyfriend and I live near.

MICHELEINE: How long have I known you? How long have I known you?

GENEVIEVE: Twenty –

MICHELEINE: – five…

GENEVIEVE: …years.

GILMA: I see my mother-in-law, her hair is on fire.

MICHELEINE: And you give up now… He will not be pleased with you… Don't blame me if Oolio's angry with you…

GENEVIEVE gathers together her coat and bag, as if preparing to go.

Genie, take your coat off.

MICHELEINE picks up a towel and rubs GENEVIEVE's hair.

GENEVIEVE: I want to be with my children. If I drive around the back road I might make the Strata route.

MICHELEINE: And you think they'll want to see you? They don't want to know you. I know, Genie, don't make us laugh any more, everyone has always known.

KATHRYN: Woman in the green dress. Almost bent double. Mouth slightly gaping as if she is going to laugh or as if she is trying not to lose the sweet out of her mouth.

Genevieve, are you alright?

GENEVIEVE nods.

(*To GILMA.*) What did she say?

GILMA: She says –

MICHELEINE: Your sons don't love you. They've lost where they've come from –

GILMA: She says –

MICHELEINE: When was the last time they even sent a card?

GILMA: She says –

GENEVIEVE: You make it hard for me to like you.

GILMA: When did you last see –

MICHELEINE: …your own grandchild.

I understand why you're angry. I understand that there is jealousy – Your husband is dead while mine is still alive. (*To KATHRYN.*) Suicide is painful.

GENEVIEVE: It wasn't suicide.

MICHELEINE: Suicide is surprising, but we weren't surprised (*To GILMA.*) Translate it.

He was a very unhappy man. (*To GENEVIEVE.*) When the inquest was called you were happy to admit this, you were happy to acknowledge that he had not been as well as before.

He had a certain darkness, a way of not seeing the world… It was irritating, destructive to say the least. I've kept the painting as a tribute to him. A reminder, that on every life some rain must fall.

(*To GILMA.*) Translate it.

GILMA: (*To KATHRYN.*) Do you understand?

KATHRYN: Yes, I understand.

MICHELEINE: He'd been depressed. It was clear he'd been depressed for a long time.

GENEVIEVE sinks into her chair. MICHELEINE comes over and takes her hand.

KATHRYN: The wife, head to head with the lady in the green dress. The loll of a scuffed sandal next to the wife's thin zebra mule.

MICHELEINE: I'm sorry. I'm sorry. Genevieve, I'm sorry, but there was nothing, nothing anyone could do.

GENEVIEVE: She calls me up, and says –

MICHELEINE: Genevieve, get your self up here –

GENEVIEVE: We have oysters to eat. There's far too many, so won't you join us. Bring…

MICHELEINE: (*To KATHRYN.*) Her husband. Her husband was a very good man.

GENEVIEVE: I leave him a note. Say come on later. He's taken our youngest son to the swimming pool. Fourteen. Darius is just fourteen.

MICHELEINE: (*To KATHRYN.*) He painted the picture, a commission for my husband. It was meant to be the most glorious view. Instead you give me polemic, instead you give me mind-numbing politics, lies. That painting lies.

GENEVIEVE: I arrive at this house and drink oysters and a liqueur. It goes to my head. I'm almost a flirt. Somebody mentions… 'Your husband is a long time.' I'm happy. Not worried. He'll be at home with the boys. And when I get home, the house is empty. The police have called. I'm to go at once. I arrive at the station to find my youngest sitting in a waiting room, holding his father's swimming towel.

He drowned. He'd been depressed. He'd taken too many… I know what pills he takes. No, you're wrong, who kills himself in view of their child? Takes and swims and drowns in view of their child. Without me even ringing them, I look up and see Micheleine and him, and I know, I see through my youngest's eyes.

MICHELEINE: If we hadn't have kidnapped you. I'm so sorry, Genie…

GENEVIEVE: My youngest wants to speak, to say something but I squeeze his hand hard –

No… I was with my friends all night long. I tell the officers. I see Oolio laughing in a back room with some officers, some brusque aside, some inside joke, about nothing, about some man who drank some magic beer and thought he was Superman, a stupid nervous joke, inappropriate yet needed, badly timed yet delivered with the telling of a raconteur, funny, making her laugh. And I know…

GILMA: I was there the day they filled in the pool.

MICHELEINE: There were no headquarters. (*Beat.*)
I suggested it one evening after supper in bed. It seemed
the only tribute to a very dear friend.

GENEVIEVE: She thinks that we admire her.

KATHRYN: In this light she is almost bearable.

MICHELEINE: By morning there were engineers knocking
down walls.

Genevieve, we're not going anywhere. We're here for the
duration.

MICHELEINE squeezes her hand, takes her coat.

You and I have nothing to be ashamed of.

KATHRYN: Your daughter? She lives on the Southside.

MICHELEINE: No matter.

KATHRYN: But your grandson?

A beat.

*MICHELEINE smoothing across the piano school, as if
ironing out a crease, she takes a seat.*

MICHELEINE: Yes, I hear what you say.

GENEVIEVE: The morning after my husband's funeral,
I sit in his studio and I look at the painting and suddenly
I see what the rest of the world can see. A frightening
view, a view of the outside. Unsettling, mocking,
outspoken, outside of what one is allowed to say and
I hear Micheleine.

MICHELEINE: But darling, where's the glorious view?

GENEVIEVE: The next day I drive the painting over to
Micheleine. 'You must have it. Please take it. He painted

it for you.' And I let them comfort me. Let them joke about his outspokenness. Because that painting frightens me, it frightens me like it did them. And from that day I am lost to my sons who see me fawn, and smile, and listen and console with these people so that they can survive. So that I…

In the distance. Shelling. Fireworks. Something. Somewhere. Very distant. Muffled by the snow and the wind and the distance.

GILMA: I look at this woman. I have her bus pass in my bag. And a lip pencil and some tweezers and a small St Christopher.

Cunt bastard's way too late.

(*Looking to KATHRYN.*) Taxi.

GILMA knocks back her coffee, slipping the cup and saucer into her bag. GILMA exits as if waiting for the taxi. MICHELEINE sits on the piano stool watching as KATHRYN packs up her equipment.

MICHELEINE: Where do you live? At home. Where is your home?

KATHRYN: I'm sorry… I don't understand what you say…

MICHELEINE: It's nice? Your home.

KATHRYN: Gilma…

MICHELEINE: And when you walk in, what do you see?

KATHRYN: I'm sorry… (*Calling out.*) Gilma? Translation please…

MICHELEINE: There is a mirror, and a table, with a key on the table and a vase of flowers, normally fresh, next to a rack of shoes –

KATHRYN: (*Calling out.*) Gilma –

GILMA smokes a cigarette, which she has only just lit, admiring the lighter, in her hand.

GILMA: My boyfriend is home on leave. We lie in bed and he pulls out the first of my grey hairs. 'Don't go too grey before I get back. Will you marry me?' Yes, I say when you come back and we have a nice house, a video, a Prada handbag. Yes, I'll marry you but looking at this boy, this soldier, with one rotten tooth, from sweet drinks when he was young. I know we won't win. I know he is no hero. I know what he does to the…my…people from the North.

MICHELEINE: When you came into my house you walked along the corridor and there are several prints, cartoons, political, mocking, which my husband likes…

KATHRYN: I don't understand you…

MICHELEINE: A bicycle is always against the door, always waiting for my complaint to Marianna who should have moved it. It is not mine. Turning left is the drawing room and to the right is reception –

KATHRYN: Gilma –

MICHELEINE: I have chosen everything in this house. Everything in this house has a place, has been chosen for a reason, everything I have formed an attachment to.

The sound of distant violence. Getting closer. GILMA as if standing in the snow, watching the distant violence coming near.

GILMA: I call out 'Kathryn'. No one hears me. The city burns now brightly. Kathryn… (*Calling out.*) Kathryn we have to go soon…

KATHRYN: They will come in this house and they will ransack it and take your things and you know what they will do to you then –

MICHELEINE: You've never looked have you? When you walk in your house, you've hardly noticed what is around, have you?

GENEVIEVE: Micheleine…

MICHELEINE: Have you?

GILMA enters.

Ask her?

There's mud on my carpet. Your shoes.

KATHRYN: What is she saying?

GILMA: She is asking about your house. The rooms.

MICHELEINE: I want to know what her house is like, she has come into mine… Ask her. Ask her.

GILMA: She says –

A beat.

KATHRYN: Hallway… Lampshade… I don't know…(*To GILMA.*) Will you tell her, I think she should leave now?

MICHELEINE: In the bedroom there's a –

KATHRYN: A bed –

MICHELEINE: (*Beat.*) That is it?

GILMA: (*To KATHRYN.*) That is it?

KATHRYN: There's a lamp and some proofs of photos that I am always about to check.

MICHELEINE: And what is on these photographs?

GILMA: The photos? By your bed?

KATHRYN: I don't want to… I don't… The massacres in the Northern states. There are several photos of children with their wounded mothers. There's a boy with his father.

GILMA: …They've cut off his hands… Some soldiers, they're taunting a local man, the local man…they're making him kill his dog.

KATHRYN: There's a small shot looks like nothing…

GILMA: Just like a puddle, it's iced over but through the water…

KATHRYN: There's a face…

GILMA: Some kid still grubby from the sandwich he was eating, the morning the soldiers came and burnt his house.

MICHELEINE: Tell her I want her to take a photograph.

GENEVIEVE: Micheleine, I'm leaving –

MICHELEINE: Tell her.

GILMA: You've to take the photo.

MICHELEINE: Tell her I want her to take the photograph of me before and after they come –

GILMA: Before and after they come…

A ricochet of noise. Muffled but nearer…

MICHELEINE: Tell her, a woman who describes her subject better than her own home, a woman with such attention to detail for her subjects, such an eye for detail, this is a woman after my own heart…

Tell her what does she have left if she doesn't have history? Tell her I'm a piece of history right under her nose.

Tell her I want her to shoot my right side, even after… My right side is the side I want the world to see…

Tell her outside of history she is nothing… A parasite… I am history… I know what I leave behind…

Tell her I want to be seated in front of the painting…
Tell her I take back nothing…

From somewhere the phone rings. And rings. And rings. And stops. Silence. GENEVIEVE picks up her coat and bag and makes to go.

Genie. Don't drip, sweetheart, you're leaving a trail of water. (*Calling after.*) Be careful. The roads are icy.

GENEVIEVE pauses, then walks over to MICHELEINE and slaps her hard across the face. A silence. GENEVIEVE turns and exits.

GENEVIEVE: (*Calling back to GILMA.*) You can have a lift if you want.

GILMA walks across the room before taking off her shoes and dumping them in the bin.

GILMA: Your shoes… A Northerner needs your shoes.

MICHELEINE: Gilma –

GILMA: A Northern name. Did I not say before?

MICHELEINE looks down at the mules on her feet, then slipping them off she holds them out to GILMA.

MICHELEINE: I think they're your size.

GILMA hesitates, then takes them, nods her thanks and exits.

KATHRYN: I am sitting in the lobby of my hotel. After. The taxi driver is arguing. He did turn up last night… He haggled about the money even when all around him…

In my wardrobe there are several packets of linen unopened. This is not some fetish just always the thing I buy. When I find myself walking aimlessly around a department store, normally en route back from some job somewhere, I always buy sheets, or pillowcases, whatever. I always buy clean white sheets. I suppose that's my whim. I take them home and am about to unpack but instead I leave them in the wrapper, for next time. I don't know why. I don't know why. Some kind of comfort I suppose. To know that somewhere they are there.

As we drive to the airport, the taxi driver curses. An old lady dances while a young soldier is shot. He is dragged through the street by a rope by his neighbours, who this week are the ones seeking revenge.

On the plane, they serve pineapple and chicken with thin chips, and for once, I am not hungry. For once I want to go…home.

A ricochet of noise. Louder. Nearer.

A window. Lamplight. The peel of an orange. The turn of the face as she stands looking out.

MICHELEINE: My face against the light. His book collection in the background. My skin. I have good skin.

(*As if seeing through a window.*) …The world is white…

KATHRYN: The hallway. The darkness. The door open outside. Outside –

MICHELEINE: The snow. Everything is…

KATHRYN: …everything is…

MICHELEINE: …stay and take your photograph

KATHRYN: …white…

MICHELEINE: What else is there to do?

The rhythmic ricochet of noise the silent undercurrent.

I am seventeen, it is snowing, I am walking back with…he's ahead of me… I tease him to hurry up, bored with his pace. He is lumbering and frightened of the ice and won't go any faster so I step across him and this time it is he who has to tiptoe behind to match my boot. And he does, laughing. It is snowing, and we are laughing. And that is when I know I have found the love of my life.

Oolio… Keep up.

KATHRYN: I'm sorry. I don't know what you're saying.

MICHELEINE turning slightly to the right.

MICHELEINE: My right side…

The ricochet of noise grows louder, carrying the ripples of violence, of shelling as KATHRYN hovers with the camera in her hand, as if holding a gun.

Shoot… Shoot…

KATHRYN hesitates then slowly aims her camera –

The End.